NEURO-ARCHITECTURE

DESIGNING HIGH-RISE CITIES AT EYE LEVEL

FRANK SUURENBROEK & GIDEON SPANJAR

nai010 publishers

FOREWORD

We are living in a period of sweeping changes. Whether it be housing, the energy transition, climate resilience, or the transition of the agricultural sector, all of these changes are having a huge impact on our living environment. The Dutch government's ambition to build almost a million homes in the next ten years and to integrate nature into the design of our society, will radically reshape our cities. How can we ensure that among the plethora of challenges we are now facing we also discover opportunities for improving our living environment?

The major transition challenges, which are driven chiefly by climate change, have a long lead time, yet they also require short-term action. Action to investigate and set in motion the necessary systems change. Action to abandon toxic practices and to translate our desire for a healthier living environment from words into deeds.

To render the long-term perspective tangible, we are going to need to draw on a combination of knowledge and imagination in an all-out effort to enthuse people about the environment of the generations to come. The huge housing construction task provides an ideal opportunity to give concrete form to these transitions: local developments meet the specific needs of a neighbourhood and contribute to the cultural development of an area. What do the people of that area really want? What are optimum conditions for developing an ecosystem that includes residents? What is required in social and physical terms to support equitable development? How will this contribute to a healthy living environment for our grandchildren?

Working towards intergenerational stewardship requires a different role of the designer. But it also involves political engagement and making better use of the typically Dutch non-hierarchical relation between client and contractor. This form of collaboration is a source of strength and opportunities. It does, however, demand both new knowhow and insights gleaned from proven design solutions already realized elsewhere in the world.

Practice-based research can play a big role here. New technologies and new fields of work offer radically different tools for spatial practice. As this book shows, the new hybrid field of neuroarchitecture has made it possible for the first time to measure and visualize how people experience their environment and architecture both physically and visually using biometric technology. It offers architects, urban planners and other designers an additional instrument for creating the right conditions for a robust urban environment.

This book about designing with the help of knowledge from neuroarchitecture is an example of the discovery and testing of possible new solutions. It is precisely these kinds of building blocks that, if we use them well, will help us to set in motion and shape the larger system transition, from bottom-up and from project to project.

Francesco Veenstra
Chief Government Architect of the Netherlands

THE
BODYGUARD
JAARBEURS

CONTENTS

PERCEPTION AS THE KEY TO THE BUILT ENVIRONMENT

We are continually and for the most part subconsciously influenced by our surroundings. Everyone has had the experience of finding themselves in a street or a square that just doesn't feel right, even though there's no immediately obvious reason. The space might be overwhelming or conversely endlessly dull. It offers few points of reference, is too cluttered or confusing. Your pace quickens, your gaze doesn't settle. Or take the opposite experience: you turn a corner and the panorama that unfolds animates, it permeates your senses. This environment stimulates and without noticing you stay there longer. Your pace is slower, more languid, your gaze more open – and you really see the surroundings.

Both experiences are key to what the design, layout and programming of our built environment is all about: creating the best possible affordances for the people who use it, spend time in it or walk through it. Until now it has not been possible to directly measure that experience. That is now changing thanks to the new emerging field of neuroarchitecture.

In recent decades considerable advances have been made in the neurosciences and environmental psychology regarding our understanding about how humans function in their environment. We now know, for example, that people are constantly scanning their surroundings; that their brain's neural network subsequently processes that visual information and that this in turn affects their behaviour and experience, usually without their being actively conscious of this.

The neurosciences are developing biometric technology and software for measuring the brain and the body's automatic responses to the environment. Neuroarchitecture harnesses that technology and knowledge for architecture and urban design. For the first time it is possible to discover how different design solutions in the built environment influence our experience, perception and behaviour. In the coming years neuroarchitecture promises to provide those involved in the construction of high-density residential environments with new tools with which to better underpin and justify their design choices.

CHALLENGES POSED BY HIGH-RISE AND DENSIFICATION

High-density, high-rise housing does not necessarily produce a strong living environment. Now that this redevelopment and densification is taking place within the existing city, it is especially important that we acquire a better understanding of the impact of high densities on people and of the role that design solutions can play. Because what we build now creates the daily environment of thousands of people for decades to come and also influences future transformations of the area. Specifically, we need to discover the impact of such redevelopment in the public space. For it is there, between the buildings, in the street, that the city's public realm is produced.

The debate about urban development is currently dominated by the dire shortage of (affordable) housing. Almost every big city is wrestling with a significant housing deficit and searching for places to build. Unlike the traditional 'horizontal' expansions of the historical city, nowadays the focus is on densifying the existing city by adding high-density housing and high-rise within the existing urban fabric.

For young professionals, students and older adults keen to live close to amenities, high densities and high-rise provide a welcome addition to the existing supply (Love et al. 2014). Moreover, inner city densification has several societal benefits. It optimizes land use in the city and safeguards the open countryside from urban development, leaving room for nature, recreation and economic activities like agricultural production. At the city level densification increases the concentration of people on a small area of land, generating economies of scale for innovative solutions for energy, mobility and waste management, and a dense network of amenities. However, the added value of this urban densification is contingent upon the creation of a high quality, healthy and attractive environment. And there lies another major challenge, not least because high-density, high-rise housing is a relatively new dwelling typology in European cities.

The scientific literature highlights multiple challenges. For example, high-rise environments are associated with social fragmentation and with the privatization of public functions. Amenities are solved in individual buildings and public functions, such as swimming pools, are withdrawn from the public domain if they are only accessible to residents (Sassen 2017). High-rise can sometimes have a negative effect on health outcomes (Lindal & Hartig 2013), with residents experiencing the surroundings as oppressive (Asgarzadeh et al. 2012). Residents in high-rise environments also have fewer opportunities for human contact and are consequently more likely to experience social isolation and loneliness (Henderson-Wilson 2008; Love et al. 2014). Direct access to dwellings from the car park renders apartment complexes anonymous and susceptible to degradation (Suurenbroek & Spanjar 2021; Arends 2023; Gifford 2007).

HIGH-RISE ON A HUMAN SCALE

Designers are aware of these potential negative effects of high-rise and densification. One frequently suggested solution is sought in a *human scale*, a concept that encapsulates the demand for a familiar, congenial and pleasant environment - despite the high densities - *between* the huge building volumes at street level. That, after all, it is where the social city is made (Sennett 2018). It is where people's daily lives play out and it is the place where densification through high-rise is most tangible. Streets are the connecting, vibrant spaces formed and bounded by buildings and by the furnishing of the street space itself. Ideally it should be an urban public realm with a mix of social and commercial uses where social interaction takes place.

POPULAR SOLUTIONS FOR A HUMAN SCALE

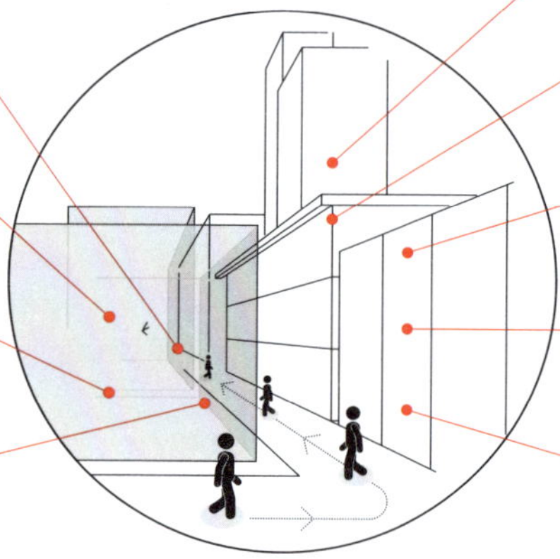

FIG. 1.1 Design solutions for a human-scaled streetscape.

Around the world, dozens of design solutions have been devised aimed at creating a human scale at street level and strengthening social amenity and walkability in the new high-density, high-rise developments. The following solutions are frequently cited [FIG. 1.1]:

- Opt for alternating horizontal and vertical blocks of varied design instead of large, monotonous blocks or stand-alone building volumes.
- Instead of placing towers flush with the street edge, incorporate them into a block that is set back from the building line.
- Keep parking out of sight of the street space as much as possible.
- Design a multi-layered and fine-grained transition and connection between private building and public street space, with differentiated elevations, entrances and the first few metres of the street space.
- Design an active base with shops and other amenities at street level so that a visual relationship is established between what happens inside the building and outside, thereby generating activity on the street and a view of the street from the buildings.
- Emphasis on a fine-grained materialization of the buildings: warm materials instead of cold concrete, and attention to detail at eye level.

However, it is essential to bear in mind that some of these design solutions are drawn from significantly different situations and cultural contexts, such as Vancouver, Toronto and New York. Moreover, the design solutions derive in part from traditional solutions in European cities. Think for example of historical centres with dense networks of streets and shops and of the districts built around the old European city centres in the late nineteenth, early twentieth century. The latter are now much-loved districts boasting a great variety of building types, with a wealth of ornamentation and detailing, that build on the accumulated architectural and urban design knowledge of earlier centuries. Whether those classic design solutions will work in the new situations of extreme densification is open to question. And what works in the Vancouver context may not necessarily be suitable in a European city.

REFERENCE LOCATIONS

Current design practice is highly diversified and unlike during the modernist period, there is no common position on urban design. What is more, construction practice is fragmented. Take the Netherlands, for example. Since the government decentralized spatial planning in 2006, responsibility for spatial development has been scattered across 352 municipalities - and in reality across the many project areas within those municipalities. The housing shortage has obviously focused attention on the volume and speed of building production, but that in turn allows relatively little opportunity to fully evaluate the reference places from which some of the human scale design principles are drawn.

Reference locations are an essential tool for understanding the envisaged effect of design decisions made during a design process based on a shared concept, knowledge and insight. Reference images have three different functions in this process. The first is to enable the client or other parties to envisage what the spatial change will look like: 'this is how you should imagine it'. The second function of reference images is to represent the task: they show the discussion partners the actual issue, rather than the solution. And thirdly, reference images refer to the accumulated knowledge of the discipline. Taking Vancouver as reference, for example, it becomes clear that while density may not be the problem, density does require a lot of the design in order to make it work spatially and socially.

MAKING HUMAN SCALE IMAGINABLE

The key question is whether, in those new high-density contexts, design solutions will actually achieve a human scale at street level from the user's perspective. Will it be experienced as such? Now that we are on the threshold of substantial densification it is essential to get a better understanding that user experience early on in the design and development process. And that is precisely where the new interdisciplinary field of neuroarchitecture offers radical new opportunities.

In this book, we introduce the concept of neuroarchitecture and connect it with research through design (an approach where designers are involved in the research process to develop practical solutions). In our practical research, we use research through design to analyse spatial designs that have already been applied in practice, using drawings. We then use neuroarchitecture to test their effect on user experience.

The structure is two-fold:
- we use **research through design** to analyse two exemplary streets and their associated design solutions in six different cities;
- we then draw on **neuroarchitecture** to chart the user experience.

Together these approaches provide insight into the design and how it works out for the users. Has it succeeded in creating a human scale? If so, how?

This book is the product of a two-year research project entitled Sensing Streetscapes (see www.building4wellbeing.com). In collaboration with a consortium of Dutch design firms, the municipality of Amsterdam, housing corporations and developers, we analysed the impact of previously implemented design solutions on the quality of the environment in general and on user experience in particular [FIG. 1.2]. In addition to drawings, sketches and design proposals, built designs provide an opportunity to consider and understand design solutions holistically. The focus is on projects that are often cited as shining examples of good design. Nevertheless, they may also have less successful aspects, and those aspects are equally instructive.

It is our hope that in the context of today's fragmented spatial practice the analyses of reference images and the registration of user experience will contribute to the creation of a shared lexicon as well as an understanding of and discussion about the different design solution options - and their consequences at eye level.

SENSING STREETSCAPES

This book presents the results of our Sensing Streetscapes research project in which an interdisciplinary team studied a number of actual streetscapes in order to discover which spatial design solutions achieve a human scale in street spaces (from building to ground plane) in densified residential areas. New knowledge, insights and technology gleaned from neuro-architecture were employed to make the design solutions measurable.

An important component of the study were the co-research sessions with the consortium partners, made up of design and consultancy agencies in the fields of urban design, architecture and landscape architecture. Together with the 'spatial clients' (local councils, housing corporations and developers) they brought their expertise and practical experience to bear in analysing the international areas with us.

During the project, a broad interdisciplinary group of experts from the neurosciences, environmental psychology and related scientific fields reflected on the research results, the methodology and the interdisciplinary challenges that this new, hybrid field of neuroarchitecture entails.

DESIGN FIRMS

SCIENTIFIC ADVISORY PANEL

SPATIAL DEVELOPMENT CLIENTS

FIG. 1.2 Consortium for the Sensing Streetscapes research project.

VIEWING AND MEASURING

The current urban densification drive is not the first time that cities have densified. We begin in chapter 2 by expanding on this. We then turn to current trends in urban housing and the new high-rise environments that are being developed. And, finally, we ask what human scale means in the new high-density contexts.

In Chapter 3 we introduce the new hybrid field of neuroarchitecture. How did it emerge, what are the key theories and technologies and what is its potential for spatial practice? We illustrate this with results of the first round of tests we conducted into existing high-rise areas in the Netherlands' three biggest cities.

What are the current trends in urban development and what kind of high-rise environments are emerging?

In Chapter 4 we subject six densification areas in six Western cities - Vancouver, Toronto, Manchester, London, Oslo and Amsterdam - to a thorough examination. In each area we analyse two typical streets with respect to the presence and effectiveness of design solutions aimed at creating a human scale at eye level. We focus specifically on the way the ground floor, the facade and the street space have been designed, and the correlation between design solutions and their actual impact on users. For the latter we complement traditional research through design with user experience as measured by our neuroarchitecture tests.

In the final chapter we synthesize the analyses into a list of the types of design solutions that can help to rescale densification to human proportions at street level.

FIG. 1.3 New high-rise in Amsterdam.
Photo: New Media Services

URBAN DENSIFICATION AND HUMAN SCALE

Cities develop in waves. This was wonderfully illustrated by the French historian Fernand Braudel in his famous 1966 study of the development of the cities and the landscape around the Mediterranean Sea. He described the backdrop of bigger – slower – developments, such as that of the landscapes and civilizations, against which more temporary and local developments play out and cities grow, stabilize, shrink and grow again. Such dynamics are also observable within a shorter timescale, which puts the current wave of urban densification into perspective.

Cities are constantly developing, both shrinking and growing over time, but they rarely disappear altogether. For example, from around 1670 the population of the once thriving Dutch city of Haarlem halved and over 1200 dwellings fell into disrepair. In 1870, after two centuries of negligible growth, Haarlem suddenly started to grow again - indeed, so rapidly that the city doubled in size in less than 25 years. The city walls were demolished, and Haarlem expanded on all sides. In no time at all flower bulb fields, workshops, gardens and pasturage on the urban perimeter were replaced by newly built neighbourhoods. Haarlem is typical of most medium-sized cities of that period.

Haarlem's growth in the late nineteenth century was fuelled by industrialization, conforming to a pattern whereby spatial developments are nearly always closely interrelated with technical and social innovations. Industrialization and socio-economic changes gave rise to a spate new spatial typologies: from shop-top housing to the new department stores, trade fair halls, 'palaces' for industry associations, and zoos. But until long after the Second World War West European cities continued to be characterized by 'horizontal' urban expansion in the form of new housing estates that conformed in size and scale to those of earlier periods. In the course of the twenty-first century the trend in Western Europe has switched from urban sprawl to the densification of the existing city through redevelopment (Cortinovis et al. 2022).

There is nothing exceptional therefore about the fact that Western cities are currently experiencing a period of growth. Nor is the huge population density anything new. At the end of the nineteenth century it was even higher owing to the mass migration of farm labourers and other country folk to the industrialized cities. Those cities took quite some getting used to with their constant hustle and bustle, and the smells and sounds of (horse-drawn) trams, steam engines and people. By contrast, the current densification of the cities is accompanied by trends aimed at making the city cleaner and healthier. Less space is being allocated to cars and the speed of automobile traffic is being reduced. New forms of transport are emerging and the transition to electric transport is expected to continue. Coincidentally, cities are becoming greener.

Also new is the trend towards high-rise - that is to say, the current form of high-rise.

MODERNIST HIGH-RISE

For centuries, West European cities have expanded horizontally by building new, low-rise districts on their urban peripheries. Space was initially restricted by the need for robust, encircling defensive works, which in many cities resulted in narrow street spaces between the blocks of buildings. In later periods footpaths appeared in these spaces, separating pedestrians from carriages and carts. Urban expansions in the nineteenth and early twentieth century still had a human scale. But that changed in the second half of the twentieth century owing to a combination of modernization, broad access to car ownership and an enormous shortage of dwellings.

It was in this period that most West European cities experienced the introduction of taller buildings. In the late 1960s in Amsterdam's south-east, construction commenced on a high-rise district in what was then polder landscape: the Bijlmermeer. The modernist masterplan by Siegfried Nassuth was intended to house 100,000 middle and working class people in 40,000 dwellings. The emphasis was on high-rise with a strict separation of working and living functions that was meant to turn Bijlmermeer into an open, green, spacious, light and healthy city. This 'functional city' concept underpinned the construction of elevated roads for rapid transit between different zones (Luijten 2002). In each of these zones, ten-storey, honeycomb-plan apartment complexes were built, surrounded by vast swathes of green space for walking and cycling.

Notwithstanding the idealistic ambitions for a healthy and attractive residential environment, the design turned out differently in practice, for a variety of reasons. The raised road network limited wayfinding, for example, and the absence of amenities, sense of 'ownership' and services in the vast green space between the buildings gave rise to a 'no man's land' plagued by public safety problems. These safety issues persisted and by 1985 a quarter of the dwellings stood empty (Luijten 2002). Bijlmermeer had quickly acquired a bad reputation. It was not until the mid-1990s, after a radical urban renewal project which saw some of the complexes replaced by clusters of 'intense low-rise' housing blocks, that the tide turned for the better.

FIG. 2.1 Bijlmermeer under construction. Source: Amsterdam City Archives

FIG. 2.2 Bijlmermeer in the 1970s. Source: Pieter Boersma photography

CONSIDERATION FOR HUMAN BEINGS AT EYE LEVEL

The modernist design dogma, which partially underpinned the Bijlmermeer, had already come under fire in other parts of the world. Well-known international experts, including Jane Jacobs, Jan Gehl, William White, Christopher Alexander and Kevin Lynch, had taken issue with the design conceived as a 'top-down compositional exercise' and argued for a human scale and for designs informed by the basic needs of the future user.

Their criticism and studies had a considerable impact on practice and have more recently spawned a new urban design paradigm (Haas 2008; Gehl 2011; Gehl & Svarre 2014; Sennett 2018). In the Netherlands, too, the focus in urban design and architecture shifted to the design of spaces with a human scale. First in the 1970s in the 'cauliflower-plan' suburbs arranged around green courts, and thereafter in the new wave of suburban development that commenced in the 1990s with the government-designated expansion areas. In essence, this amounted to the rediscovery and redeployment of classic town planning design solutions (Haas 2008; Sim 2019).

Part of this new paradigm is the renewed interest in designing urban blocks with street space between the buildings. This street conceived as place is the product of the configuration, composition, programming and materialization of the buildings and the ground plane. The urban design discipline and the social sciences have conducted extensive research into the role of public space in the social city - and of how it provides opportunities for frequent encounters and is consequently essential to ensure trust between strangers. Public spaces like city parks, squares and city streets have a role to play as vital breeding places for the social city. The design creates the conditions for this.

What characterizes most of these studies - including pioneering studies like those of Alexander, Gehl and Allan Jacobs - is a focus on the historical city centres and other places that are already fairly successful. Although public space in ordinary residential areas and elsewhere also possesses public realm qualities, they get much less attention (see also: Suurenbroek et al. 2019). Let alone how these qualities are being translated into a new housing typology that is gaining in popularity in the current high-rise redevelopment in city centres: that of the hybrid urban block.

THE NEW HYBRID URBAN BLOCK

Urban housing has almost imperceptibly entered upon a new phase. Projects are making a considerable leap in scale in terms of planning areas in the context of the redevelopment of existing (industrial) work and peripheral zones. Here, in the midst of a sprawling network of anonymous roads, dark and windy desolation, far from the city centre and devoid of amenities, people are suddenly supposed to start living. That places enormous demands on the design of the first complexes. A new building typology is emerging at the interface between architecture and urban design, that of the hybrid urban block: a combination of a semi-closed block and several apartment towers. Set atop an urban base that is governed by specific rules, the blocks are shaped by a number of architectural solutions at the level of the building. The illustration below depicts several examples of the type.

What these examples show are the high densities of the complexes, expressed as a Floor Space Index between 4 and almost 8. The spatial structure is relatively simple: closed or semi-closed block + apartment towers = hybrid urban block. The design is then guided by a set of parameters. In addition to ensuring solar access, the challenge is to combine facilities like car and bicycle parking and garbage, creating a multi-storey podium and a network of greenspace and meeting places inside, outside, on the street, in the courtyard and on the upper floors. Living, working, social housing and mid-priced rental are mixed together in different configurations. There are also design rules at the level of the block aimed at creating an attractive environment, such as differences in material use, active ground floors, variation in heights and widths, use of greenery in the internal courtyards and beyond, and recently even (partially) on the elevations and the upper floors.

The design of these hybrid urban blocks is occasionally done by a single architectural firm, but it is more often a joint effort by several firms each designing architectural solutions for individual plots. The unifying concept for a good environment is a human scale at street level. But what is a human scale in this new kind of context?

Having studied the new area and building designs and conducted interviews with urban planning directors of the largest Dutch cities, we can identify a number of design strategies that are aimed at achieving a human scale (Suurenbroek & Spanjar 2021). They fall into two categories: scaling and activation at eye level.

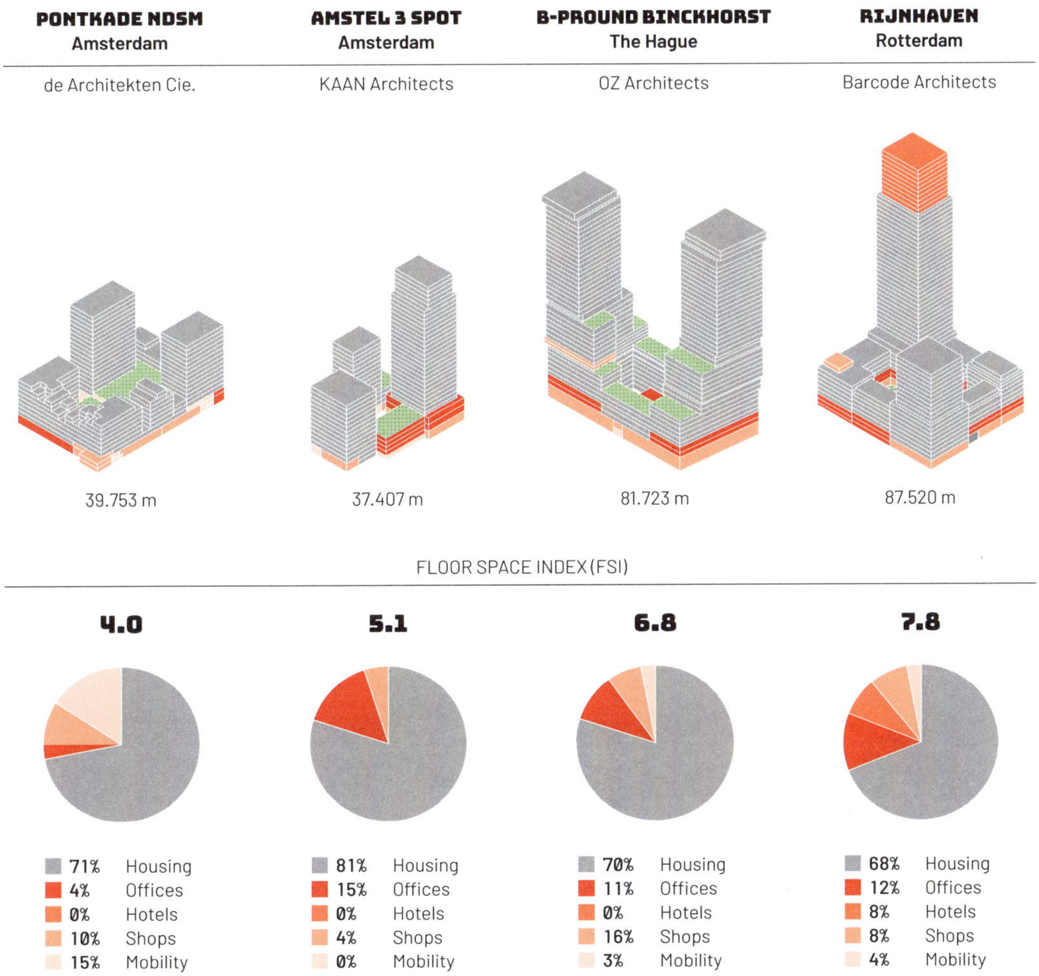

FIG. 2.3 Examples of the hybrid urban block.
Source: More Architecture for the Chair of Spatial Urban Transformation

SCALING AS A STRATEGY FOR A HUMAN SCALE

Scaling relates to interventions that render the visual bulk of high-rise more human by reducing it to more acceptable proportions on the street-facing side. Examples include the use of setbacks, where the tower is placed slightly back from the building line rather than landing unmediated on the street. Part of this strategy involves working with a standard height that is in harmony with that of existing buildings, which serves to balance the height to width ratio of the streets. Interestingly, the standard height can differ from one city to another. The average height of urban development in Utrecht, for example, is lower than that in Rotterdam.

Alongside making the building seem lower on the street-facing side, there is a parallel strategy of drawing elements of public outdoor space into the complex. Examples include a series of roof gardens and the creation of a central courtyard. The most effective size and scale for such interventions is yet to be established. A wide variety can already be found in a few recent Dutch examples (see figure 2.3). Shared outdoor space and gardens on upper floors continue to predominate in the plans, but their actualization, effect and practical value yet to become apparent in practice.

Scaling is achieved by ceasing to design the blocks as monolithic entities and instead working with a more small-scale subdivision.

Related to scaling is the introduction of more vertical greenery, which makes the building 'softer' and accords with ideas about the restorative value of greenery for the residents. The Italian architect Stefano Boeri played a pioneering role here with his 2014 Bosco Verticale building in Milan. It consists of two apartment towers of 110 and 76 metres (360 and 294 ft) respectively, whose elevations are entirely planted with trees and shrubs.

Bosco Verticale has inspired many developments, including the 2021 Trudo Toren in Eindhoven, whose nineteen floors are planted with 125 trees, and the forthcoming Wonderwoods in Utrecht, consisting of two greened towers of approximately 73 and 105 metres (239 and 344 ft). MVRDV's The Valley (2022) in Amsterdam's Zuidas (see Chapter 4) features a new typology that combines greening with a new interpretation of the human scale in high-rise. The Valley combines mirrored glass elevations that refer to the district's business identity and brick elevations that appear to have been carved out of rock. The apartments have terraces planted with a total of 200 trees and plants whose selection was overseen by renowned garden architect Piet Oudolf. Scaling is achieved here by breaking up the usual monotonous block into smaller-scale elements that vary in height and width. This is in fact a return to the classic strategies that have been used in cities for centuries. In some cases the construction is 'separated' from the facade.

Finally, the interventions are also supposed to contribute to the further scaling of the blocks by avoiding downdraughts or finding clever ways of letting sunlight into the block.

EYE-LEVEL DESIGN AS A STRATEGY FOR A HUMAN SCALE

The practice of focusing on the city at eye level has an even longer history than scaling. In particular, the importance of the ground floor of buildings and other transitional zones is universally acknowledged. Karsenberg et al. (2020) is a recent practical study in which the quality of the street-level interface is extensively explored and illustrated with examples. Like most other recent studies, the book is indebted to the classic studies that were the first to refocus on the human element in the design. Kevin Lynch, for example, claimed that pedestrians benefit from well-defined and clearly expressed ground floors and that people enjoy the spaces where such street fronts exist (1960). Alexander, Ishikawa & Silverstein (1977) followed with their own groundbreaking *Pattern Language* in which they stressed the importance of ground floors and facades in creating welcoming and inviting places that people enjoy visiting. Jan Gehl in his *Cities for People* (2010) and his partner David Sim (2019) have suggested that high quality ground levels and well-designed elevations draw visitors and create desirable public spaces. A lot of attention is paid to materialization, form and rhythm, often expressed in terms of what not to do.

The allure that street edges exert on the human eye are part of our evolutionary consciousness (Sussman & Hollander 2015, Chapter 2). Street edges are currently regarded as an essential component of the design task (Glaser 2012; Dovey & Wood 2015; Thwaites et al. 2020). The street edge is the physical space where the building makes contact with the street space. The ground floor is part of that, but the space is wider and also includes the 'encroachment' or 'transitional' zone. Glaser (2012) has shown how street edges determine the general ambience of streets. Human experiences of street edges turn out to be influenced by both the physical expression and the design and by human presence itself. Street edges are socio-spatial domains (Thwaites et al. 2013; Dovey & Wood 2015; Simpson 2018). Simpson et al. (2019a; 2019b) observed that street edges attract the most visual attention compared with other parts of the street.

Obviously street edges are not alone in determining human experience of the street. Greenery plays an important role, too, and that is just the beginning. Urban ambitions regarding bio-diversity enhancement, climate adaptation and a healthier and more sustainable city are currently generating new public space interventions that also affect the perspective at eye level: car-free streets and greening. Well-known examples include the radical greening plans for the Avenue des Champs-Élysées in Paris and the Superilla project in Barcelona, a superblock strategy where traffic is limited in order to free up public space. Similar plans are in the making in the Netherlands as well. Rotterdam, for example, has radical greening plans.

In area development greenery has recently been applied according to the 'Plaza strategy' that is based on the New York practice of balancing densification with more public space. In the case of new developments, the addition of greenery on the street side of the site can be stipulated in the tender process. Or the developer can build higher in exchange for good quality semi-public green space within the property lines. In places like Amsterdam-Zuidas (see Chapter 4) and Amsterdam-Zeeburg, this strategy has resulted in increasing numbers of pocket parks between building and street space. Another recent development is the transition to nature-inclusive area development in which the focus is on developments that take the underlying ecosystem into account.

Greenery softens the transition while simultaneously increasing the visual distance between building and street. The question is whether this impacts on the 'eyes on the street' aspect described by Jane Jacobs (1961) and how exactly it influences the visual and general experience of the user at street level. A second tactic is to greatly reduce the presence of the car in the streetscape. This takes several forms. One decades-old strategy is to banish the majority of parking underground or elsewhere out of sight. Another way of reducing the dominance of motorized traffic for pedestrians involves drastically reducing the speed limit and regulating vehicular accessibility. This considerably reduces the disparity between the speed of cars and the vigilance demanded of pedestrians. There are also more radical solutions as in Barcelona where the car has been banned from part of the public space. This is in the aforementioned Superilla project where it has been calculated that the city can double the space allocated to cycle paths and greenery and, in the process, create room for electric charging, water harvesting and other major projects.

MAKE IT MEASURABLE?

Whether the combination of design solutions can deliver a human scale at the level of scale of the street in high-rise environments is still open to question. Most of the design solutions have their origins in very different contexts, such as nineteenth-century European cities and international model reference locations like Vancouver and London. For the first time, the new field of neuroarchitecture offers the opportunity to actually measure the impact and so develop a more evidence-based design approach. What exactly neuroarchitecture is and where its roots lie is the subject of the next chapter.

NEURO-ARCHITECTURE: HOW IT WORKS AND ITS POTENTIAL

Our brains are extremely efficient when it comes to processing information. In simple terms that efficiency means that we are not always actively aware of the processes our brains carry out. It often happens subconsciously. Our brains 'disturb' us as little as possible, which is why we generally react to situations instinctively or intuitively. Take walking. We don't have to think about it. We do it automatically: we activate the muscles to lift the leg, to bring the foot forward, to land, unroll and position our mass correctly to retain our balance. Yet this everyday action requires complex control on the part of our brain and a concerted response of by the body's systems. The lengthy process and immense perseverance required to learn to walk again after a serious accident is testament to that. It would be impossible to act if we were continually aware of all the processes taking place in our brains and our bodies.

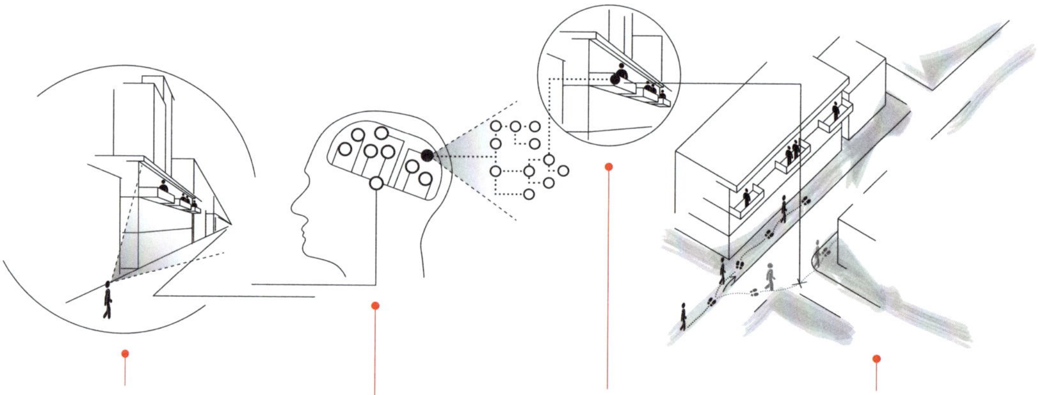

WE CONSTANTLY (SUBCONSCIOUSLY) SCAN OUR ENVIRONMENT

FIG. 3.1 Processing information from scanning the street: the senses absorb information that is processed by the brain, influencing people's walk, behaviour and perception.

When we are outdoors, we are continually scanning the environment in search of information. Sometimes that is conscious, as when we search for wayfinding aids, such as a zebra crossing where we can safely cross the road. But more often than not we are unaware of our scanning behaviour. What we observe is processed at lightning speed by our brains and influences our subsequent behaviour. Based on the information our brain absorbs from our senses, we change direction, quicken our pace in the presence of danger or slow down when we encounter an interesting place. And all that processed information contributes to our perception of the situation and the place [FIG.3.1].

The design of the place plays a major supporting role, both in the extent to which we are able to carry out certain activities like finding our way, and in our general well-being. So what exactly is the impact of the (densified) built environment on human beings and how can we enhance that impact with the right design solutions?

Until recently spatial designers relied on traditional forms of research for feedback on their design proposals whereby user experiences and needs are gauged via surveys, interviews and participation sessions. Unfortunately, there is a discrepancy between what people say they see, hear, feel and think, and their actual experience. Even the user is not always aware of this, which helps explain the disappointment people often feel when confronted with the end result. Neuroarchitecture allows us for the first time to measure (evidence-based) how users consciously and subconsciously experience a place and to see what role architecture plays and, more importantly, might play in this.

EMERGING TECHNOLOGY

The new hybrid field of neuroarchitecture takes knowledge and technology garnered from the neurosciences and environmental psychology and applies it to the architectural domain in order to measure the impact of architectural design solutions on the brain and the central nervous system in order to better understand human behaviour. One of the driving forces in this field is the Academy of Neuroscience for Architecture (ANFA). Founded in 2002 at the celebrated Salk Institute in San Diego [FIG. 3.2], its mission is to promote neuroscience research in order to gain a better understanding of human responses to the built environment. Architects are part of this multidisciplinary group, and they use the accumulated knowledge to improve spatial design. Neuroarchitecture is currently engaged in acquiring insights into how architecture is experienced by human beings by monitoring the body's reaction to a wide variety of stimuli from the built environment.

FIG. 3.2 Academy of Neuroscience for Architecture (ANFA), part of the Louis Kahn designed Salk Institute in San Diego. Source: Eric Rubens

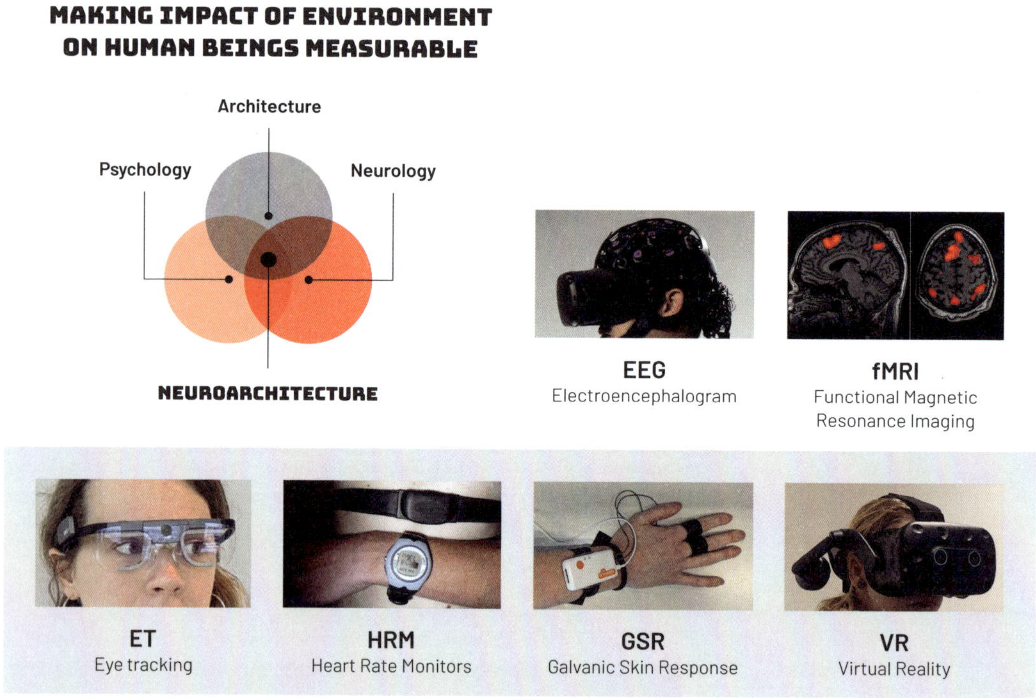

FIG. 3.3 Emerging biometric technology.

New and existing techniques, such as the electroencephalogram (EEG), Functional Magnetic Resonance Imaging (fMRI), eye tracking (ET), Galvanic Skin Response (GSR) and Heart Rate Monitors (HRM), offer new biometric methods for directly measuring the impact of a built environment design on its users from the moment their senses register that information [FIG. 3.3].

The new-generation EEG is mobile and can measure brain activity in real time. The technique reveals how various spatial features trigger fluctuations in specific brainwaves (see also Karandinou & Turner 2017). One example of an important brainwave pattern is frontal alpha asymmetry (FAA), which is defined as the difference between right and left alpha activity across frontal regions of the brain. It provides an objective measure of the propensity to exhibit approaching versus withdrawing behaviour. A strong FAA may signify a positive feeling about the urban environment and situation (see Olszewska-Guizzo et al. 2020).

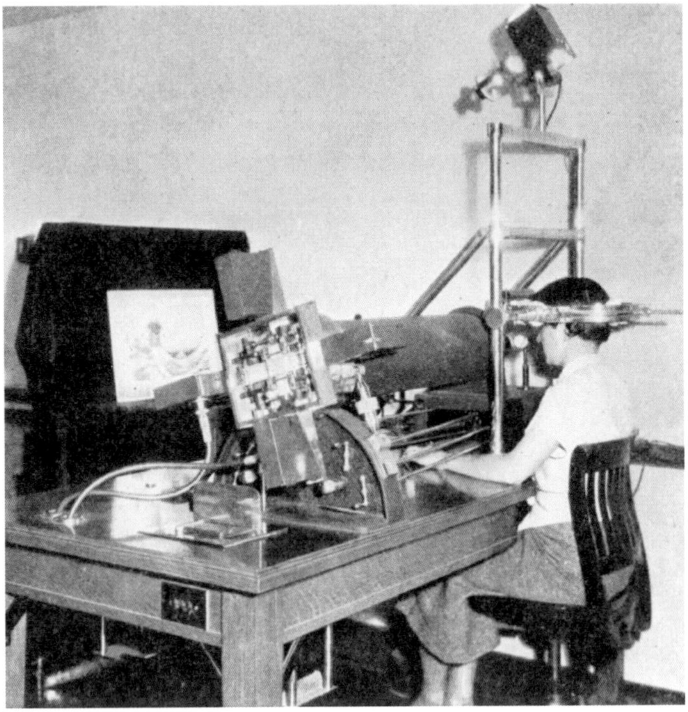

FIG. 3.4 One of the first eye-tracking machines, developed by Thomas Buswell in 1935.
Source: Buswell, G.T. (1935). *How People Look at Pictures. A Study of the Psychology of Perception in Art*, Chicago: University of Chicago Press

Functional Magnetic Resonance Imaging (fMRI) measures the slight changes in blood flow that occur with brain activity. It produces a 3D image of the brain in which the active parts of the brain light up in response to the flow of oxygen-rich blood. By presenting participants with photos of different urban situations it is possible to see what brain activity patterns they trigger (see Bermudez et al. 2017). GSR and HRM have been used experimentally to detect the stress and emotional excitement evoked by some urban situations (see Hollander et al. 2022).

GSR measures the body's sweat output, however minimal, through sensors fitted around the index and middle fingers. When someone is exposed to a positive or negative emotional experience their body sweats more and their heart rate increases. The latter can be measured using HRM (Hollander et al. 2022). GSR is a valuable addition to other technologies like eye tracking.

Eye tracking (ET) is the most developed of these technologies and the most applicable to neuroarchitecture. In ET sensors are simultaneously focused on the eye and the environment and they measure exactly where someone looks. ET has a long history. The first prototype, developed in 1935 by Thomas Buswell, was used to discover what people looked at when viewing paintings [FIG. 3.4]. Since then ET technology has undergone considerable refinement and optimization.

Eye movements can now be tracked by an ET bar attached to a computer screen; there is also a mobile version in the form of spectacles with integrated eye sensors and cameras. ET is used a lot in e-marketing to test and improve website interfaces in real time. The technology is also used for neuromarketing purposes in relation to film trailers and advertisements. This biometric technology shows promise in the testing of spatial and health hypotheses, theories and design solutions and the relationship between human beings and the environment.

In eye tracking, sensors focused simultaneously on the eye and the surroundings measure exactly what the individual is looking at.

At the end of the twentieth century, Rachel and Stephen Kaplan from the University of Michigan and Roger Ulrich from Chalmers University of Technology in Gotenburg devised groundbreaking health studies aimed at interpreting psychological reactions to our environment. According to their overlapping Attention Restoration Theory (Kaplan & Kaplan 1989; Kaplan 1995) and Psycho-Evolutionary Theory (Ulrich 1984), looking at nature can have restorative health effects, and nature in general is more highly valued by human beings than an urban environment. These findings mesh with studies carried out by E.O. Wilson in which he observed that people have an innate interest in nature, react positively to it and feel an affinity with it because that is where their genetic origins lie (1984; 1995). Wilson's biophilia hypothesis is now finding expression in Biophilic architecture, in which nature is interwoven with the building, as in green facades (see Chapter 2), with a view to having a positive effect on the health of the user.

EYE TRACKING ARCHITECTURE

Of all these technologies, eye tracking and the accompanying software is sufficiently developed to be used to investigate the impact of the built environment on people. Over the past millennia human beings have prioritized the visual sense to the extent that it is now crucial when moving through urban environments. It is surmised that in highly densified locations high-rise plays an important role in visual perception, but the precise level of that impact is unknown. Now the effects on pedestrians of design solutions aimed at scaling high-rise, such as setbacks, can be measured with the help of advanced eye tracking technology.

This is how it works. Thirty times a second the eye tracker records the exact direction of a person's gaze and all their eye movements. This then generates an accurate image of viewing behaviour. The technology enables us to distinguish some one hundred parameters related to eye movements (Holmqvist et al. 2011) ranging from fixations and fixation duration to the distances travelled by the eye. This makes it possible to separate actual visual perception from subjective evaluations of a place, and that information can be passed on to policy makers and designers.

In order to evaluate how we respond to urban situations psychologists often use nature as a reference area. When test subjects look at urban environments, their visual scanning behaviour, measured in terms of eye travel distances, is on average more rapid and the duration of their fixations shorter than in natural environments (Valtchanov & Ellard 2015; Berto et al. 2008). An acceleration of eye movements, short fixation duration and blinking all point to more cognitively demanding processing (Holmqvist et al. 2011, Franěk et al. 2018). The clear difference in eye-movement patterns patterns as measured in urban and natural settings can be explained by the level of visual complexity. Natural environments consist of moderate levels of complexity that attract our attention and fascinate us in a 'soft' way. The built environment by contrast can be quite complex and hard so that it is more difficult to capture and retain our attention (Van Den Berg et al. 2016; Nadal et al. 2010; Valtchanov & Ellard 2015; Franěk et al. 2018).

COGNITIVE PROCESSING OF INFORMATION

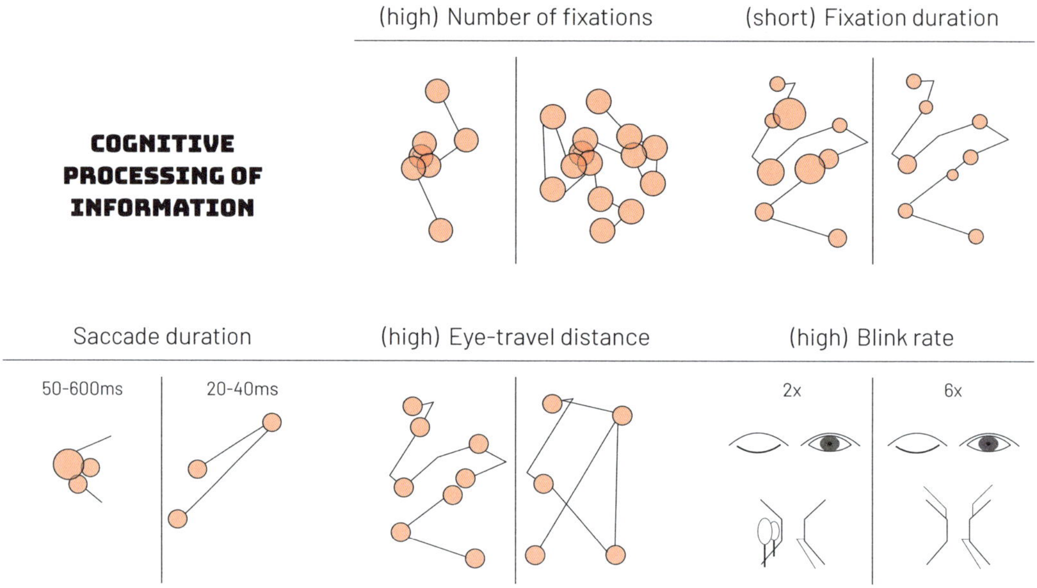

FIG. 3.5 Processing information from normal situations left, and from more complex situations right.

When our senses are over-stimulated, we have great difficulty processing all the information we receive. In such situations, handling additional calls on our cognitive capacity and holding a conversation at the same time is almost impossible. Our gaze darts from one object to another and our blink rate increases. This kind of behaviour can be caused by the environment and/or the situation. Take an extreme example like a busy street where you are trying to locate a particular shop while manoeuvring your way through a crowd. The multiplicity of elements in the street space and the obtrusive advertising, flags and lettering along the street front create a complex situation for our brains, making it difficult to process properly. The resulting visual behaviour is characterized by a high number of very short fixations and long eye-travel distances [FIG. 3.5]. This can indicate a high cognitive load, making it difficult for our brains to process the information we are trying to glean from an environment or situation (Valtchanov & Ellard 2015; Franěk et al. 2018).

In such situations individual elements are easily overlooked, as ET research carried out in the H-Buurt in Amsterdam's Bijlmermeer demonstrated (see also Chapter 2). When you exit the Bullewijk metro station you find yourself opposite the Heesteveld urban renewal location where an array of colours, forms and signs vie for your attention, which helps to explain why test subjects failed to see a five-metre-all black pole in the foreground (Suurenbroek & Spanjar 2018; 2021).

Because people subconsciously try to read situations rapidly, they search for patterns in the architecture of buildings and in the street space that help them process a lot of information efficiently. Complex, cluttered environments have a disruptive effect. Conversely, a certain amount of complexity is necessary to establish a connection with the environment. Research has shown that people confronted with a blank wall search uneasily for something interesting to fasten on and to talk about (Ellard 2015). They perceived the streetscape as monotonous and felt bored and discontented. A GSR measurement also revealed a low level of stimulation.

There are three types of complexity: (1) diversity and the number of elements in the environment, (2) symmetry and (3) the way elements are organized, i.e. whether they are perceived as an integrated whole (Nadal et al. 2010). Urban environments with variation offer opportunities for visual exploration and discovery and people regard them as healthier (Lindal & Hartig 2013). It is easier to absorb the streetscape and the facade details, and the variation in the street space generates an atmosphere that evokes a 'sense of being away' from one's usual thoughts and concerns (Lindal & Hartig 2013).

The viewing behaviour is reflected in a high number of fleeting eye fixations and long travel distances.

So the level of complexity and variation is crucial to the extent to which the user establishes a connection with the environment (see also Simpson 2018) and to how the interchange between user and environment plays out (Mallgrave 2013). In very high-density locations architects and urban designers try to respond with specific design solutions. To what degree those design solutions contribute to an agreeable level of complexity and variation in densified residential areas and what exactly it is they do to facilitate, support and connect the pedestrian were explored in a preliminary experiment.

TESTING TECHNOLOGY AND DEVELOPING METHODOLOGY

The use of eye tracking to measure the effect on people's visual experiences of design solutions in high-rise environments is still in the initial stages of development. How can visual experiences of different environments be compared and how can those disparate experiences be traced back to design solutions? To answer those questions we selected fifteen streetscapes in post-1990 high-rise environments in Amsterdam, Rotterdam and The Hague where the architecture exhibits three 'classic' design solutions: an active ground floor, rhythm and variation in the street edges, and tactile materials.

The viewer's distance from the buildings plays an important part in how they are perceived.

To imitate the pedestrian's perspective for the purposes of the study, we devised a photographic protocol that served as the basis for creating the streetscapes. Drawing on the findings of Gehl (2011), who posited that the distance to buildings and elements of the street space play a key role in people's experience and perception, we selected 'far away' and 'close by' viewpoints. From the 'far away' viewpoint 14-23 metres away from the buildings, people are able to see the entire contour of buildings, even tall ones, whereas from 'close by', walking on the footpath alongside a building (0-5 metres away), they experience the relationship between interior and exterior and between the height and width of a street [FIG. 3.6]. The photos were taken at the eye level of the average Dutch citizen, in dry weather conditions, and were not digitally manipulated.

In the test, a panel of fourteen spatial experts from the Sensing Streetscapes [FIG. 1.2] consortium (see box) was asked to rank each photo on the presence and quality of three design solutions: active ground floor, rhythm and variation (horizontal-vertical), tactility of materials. Drawing on their different expertise in architecture, landscape architecture, spatial planning and urban design, the streets were then evaluated on the basis of consensus [FIG. 3.7].

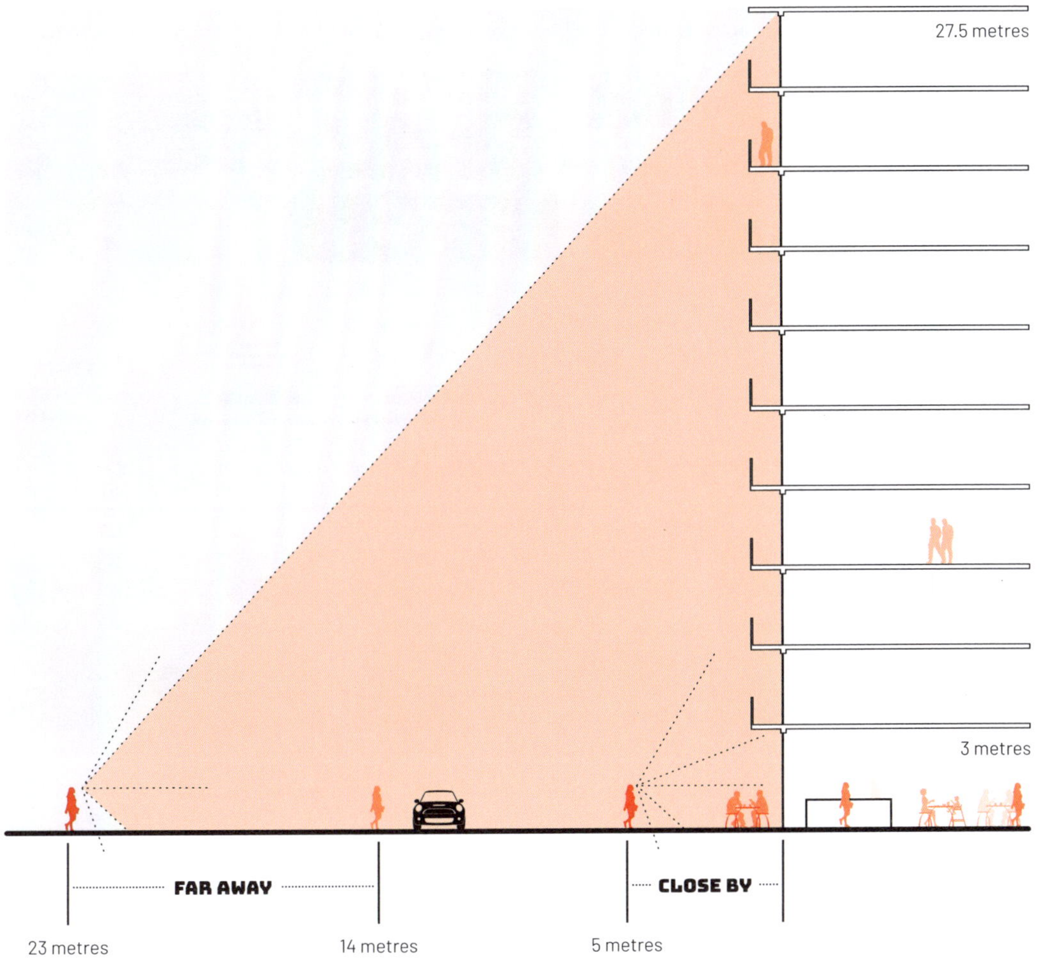

FIG. 3.6 The 'far away' and 'close by' viewpoints were based on the difference in experience and perception of the pedestrian. Adaptation of Gehl et al. 2006.

Once the spatial experts had completed their assessment of the streetscapes, the neuroarchitecture test was set up. A Tobii x2-30 compact eye-tracking bar was placed in a closed space and 31 randomly chosen students from the Amsterdam University of Applied Sciences acted as test participants. They wore noise-cancelling headphones to minimize distracting noise. Once the eye-tracking device had been calibrated, they were instructed to 'adopt an open attitude to the environment they were going to see'. The streetscapes appeared on a screen in a slide show, with each image being presented for five seconds. The first seconds are the most important for recording people's subconscious scanning behaviour. After each image, the statement 'I would like to walk along this street' appeared on the screen and participants gave their opinion on a scale of 1 to 5 [FIG. 3.7].

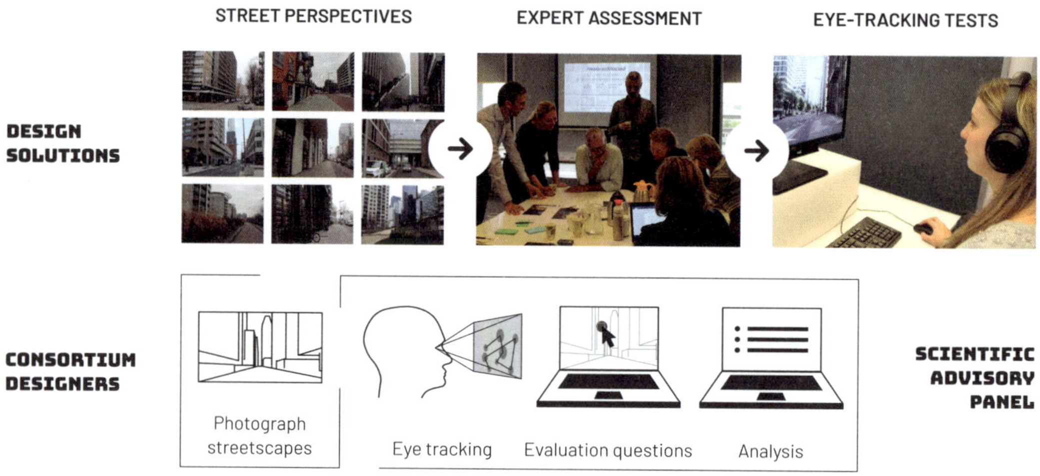

FIG. 3.7 Methodology development.

FIG. 3.8 Building a heatmap from an aggregation of viewing behaviour.

The viewing behaviour was then analysed using Visual Attention Software (iMotions), rendered as heatmaps and gazepaths.

The heatmap represents an aggregation of the viewing behaviour of all 31 participants. The software overlays the image with a grid in which the value of each square represents the relative intensity of the tracked gaze. The squares with the highest values vis-à-vis other squares are coloured red/yellow ('hot'), while the other squares, which were seen but by fewer participants and/or less intensively, are coloured green ('cold') [FIG. 3.8]. In addition to this aggregation of eye-movement patterns during the full five seconds, the data is also depicted second by second. This provides insight into the dynamics of eye movements [FIG. 3.9].

Sometimes you may want to analyse the scanning behaviour of individual participants, for example because you want to know the starting and ending points, and the path the eye travels in between the two. What immediately catches the attention and what do people not look at?

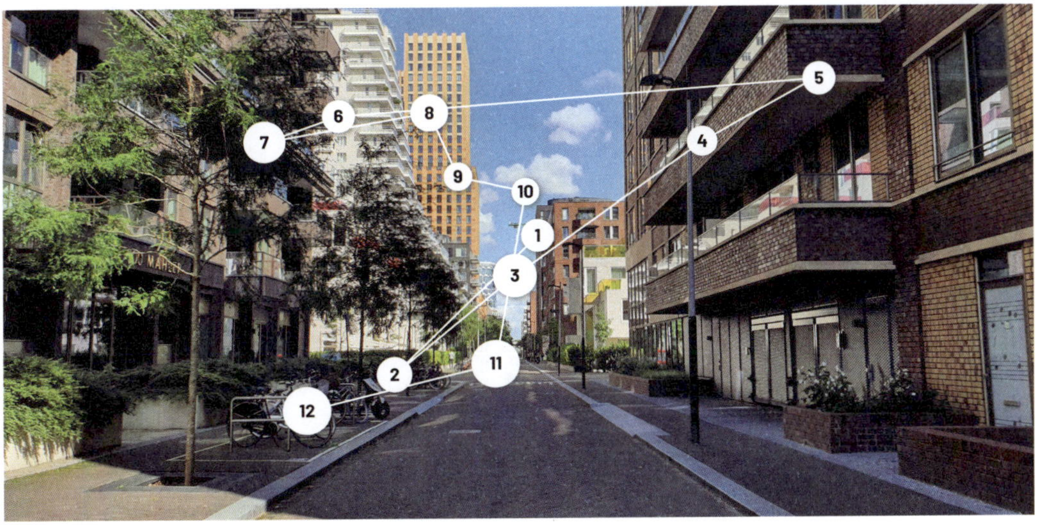

FIG. 3.9 Heatmap of George Gershwinlaan representing 2-3 seconds of aggregated eye movements of 31 research participants.

FIG. 3.10 Gazepath of George Gershwinlaan showing the path followed by the eye of a single research participant.

This information is captured by 'gaze mapping', which in this case visualized the sequence of eye fixations throughout the five seconds spent looking at each individual image. The gaze path is represented by lines and the sequence of eye fixations by numbered circles. This makes it possible to see the precise moment when the brain of each individual had difficulty processing the incoming information (fixation duration, travel distance, etc.) and what they were focusing at that moment [FIG. 3.10] Such an analysis provides instructive insights into people's behaviour in and perception of an urban environment.

EYE-MOVEMENT PATTERNS AND PRELIMINARY FINDINGS

We illustrate the potential lessons from this test with a brief comparative analysis of four European streetscapes with similar viewpoints and spatial conditions [FIG. 3.11].

The four streets were chosen in collaboration with our consortium partners (practising designers) who agreed that while the first **Street A** had an active ground floor, it was nevertheless considered anonymous because of the lack of variation and rhythm and the research participants' assessment was mostly neutral. In the first half second people fixated on the left-hand ground floor in the background, where roof and elevation converge. Shortly thereafter signs and a display mannequin caught their attention, after which they looked at buildings on the other side of the street.

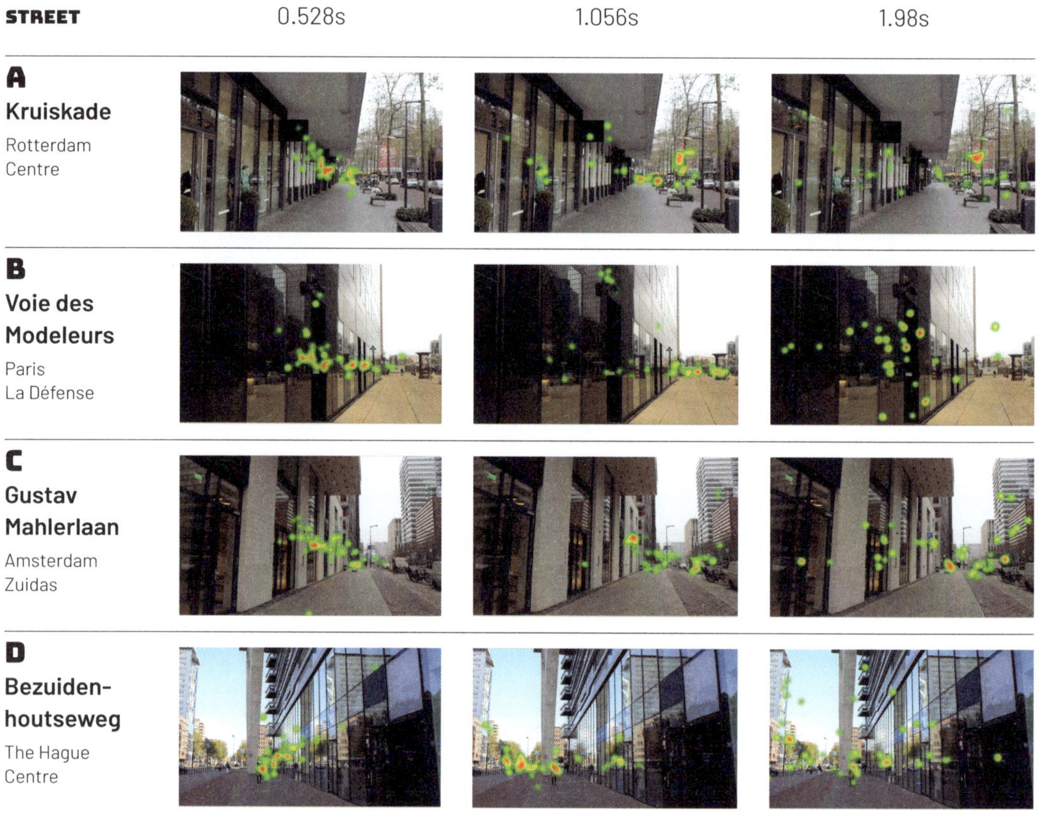

FIG. 3.11 Four streets with comparable viewpoints and spatial settings showing eye-movement patterns of 31 participants in three time frames. Source: Spanjar & Suurenbroek 2020

The experts agreed that **Street B** did not have an active ground floor. They described the facade and the street space as 'monotonous', with little variation or use of tactile materials. The research participants were asked whether they agreed with the statement that they would like to walk down this street. Their responses were mixed: 9 agreed, 2 agreed strongly, 7 disagreed and 13 were neutral. In the first half second the openings on the ground floor immediately drew their attention. This was followed by scanning of the street space and fixations on the sole pedestrian and the only signboard, after which their gaze returned to the openings in the building and reflections of the street space. The lack of variation here allowed little scope for visual exploration and is in line with the findings of Lindal & Hartig (2013).

The experts could not agree whether the building in the foreground of **Street C** had an active ground floor, but all concurred on the vertical rhythm and the presence of tactile material in the street space. Around half the participants liked this tableau and the other half were neutral, with the exception of one negative reaction. In the first half second participants focused on the ground floor, then, later, on the end of the street and on various signs.

In **Street D** the experts agreed that there was no variation in the ground floor or in the streetscape. They felt that the height of the ground floor made it difficult to create a human scale. The participants were positive about this streetscape: 21 agreed with the statement that they would like to walk along this street, 2 agreed strongly, 7 were neutral and 1 disagreed. The smooth material used for the facade of this building reflected the blue sky and immediately attracted the attention of several participants; this was followed by a pattern of eye movements along the ground floor, past the pedestrian in the image and to the end of the street. Interestingly, whether a ground floor is transparent or closed has little effect on eye fixation: rhythm disappears, and facades only attract attention with openings or reflections (see Street B).

FIG. 3.12 George Gershwinlaan was also highly rated by the experts. Source: New Media Services

The preliminary results appear to demonstrate that the streetscapes in which all three design solutions had been applied tended to attract people's visual attention. In the George Gershwinlaan [FIG. 3.12], for example, participants focused on the ground floor and on variation in the facade, such as the bay windows and balconies – what Jane Jacobs dubbed 'eyes on the street' back in 1961. The spatial experts praised the level of detail in these streets: the paving stones, for example, generate a small scale and the greenery in the primary visual field softens the high-rise. It is hardly surprising therefore that of the twelve selected streets Gershwinlaan was the most highly rated by the participants.

The absence of the three design solutions, such as an active ground floor, resulted in many more searching eye-movement patterns. The results partially accord with a previous finding that detailed buildings are viewed for longer (Van Den Berg et al. 2016).

We used this initial experimental test as the basis for the following study of international urban areas, while continuing to refine the methodology and technology. (For more information about this initial test and findings see: Spanjar & Suurenbroek 2020).

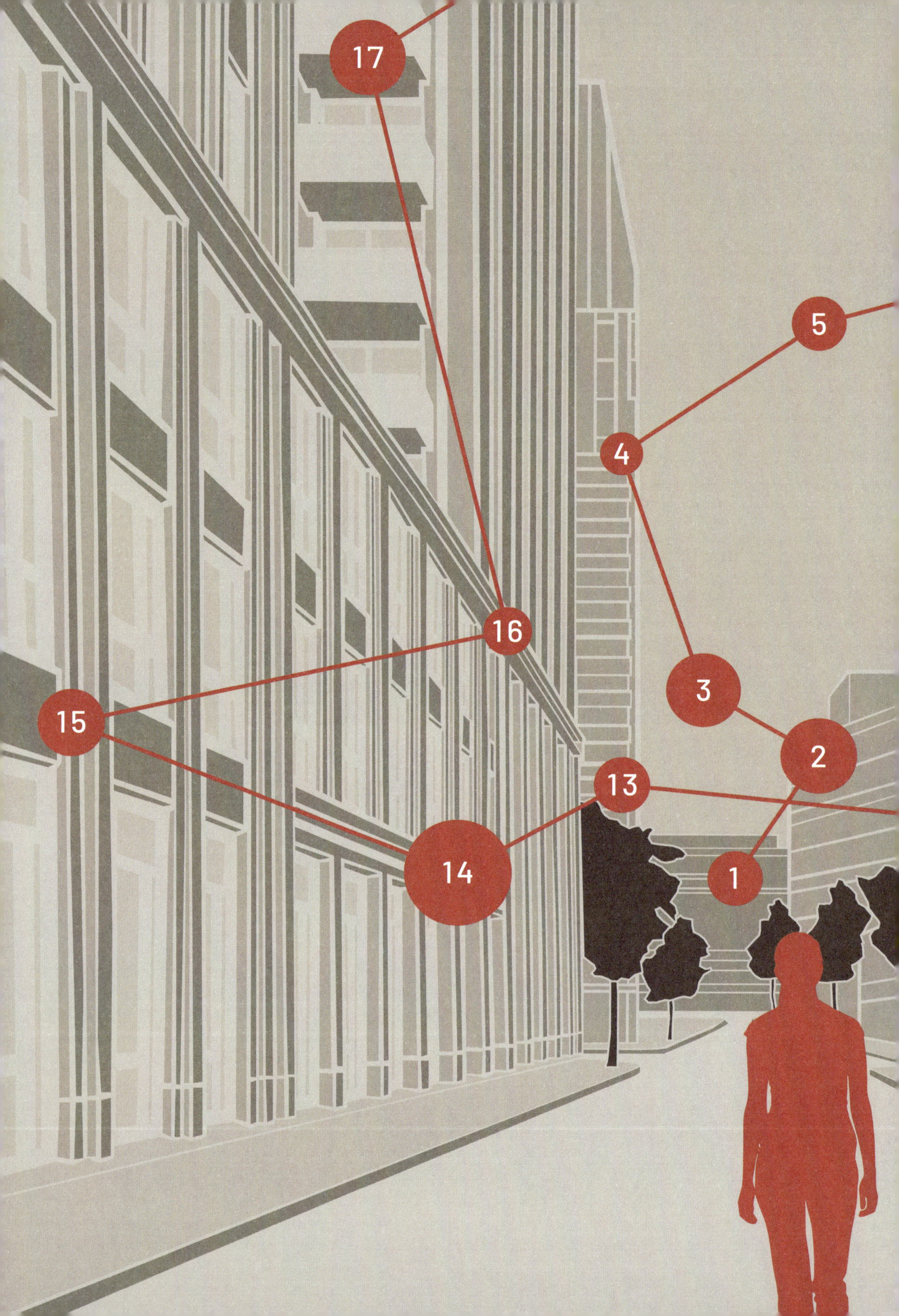
17
5
4
16
3
15
2
13
14
1

EXEMPLARY STREETSCAPES IN HIGHLY URBANIZED CITIES

In this chapter we analyse a total of twelve streets in six different areas. We selected these locations in collaboration with our Sensing Streetscapes consortium of spatial design experts [FIG. 1.2]. The streets are located in six international cities that are often referenced in the context of Dutch urban densification plans. Within those cities we looked for high-density areas where the buildings exceed thirty metres (98 feet) in height and several of the design solutions associated with a human scale are present or, totally absent.

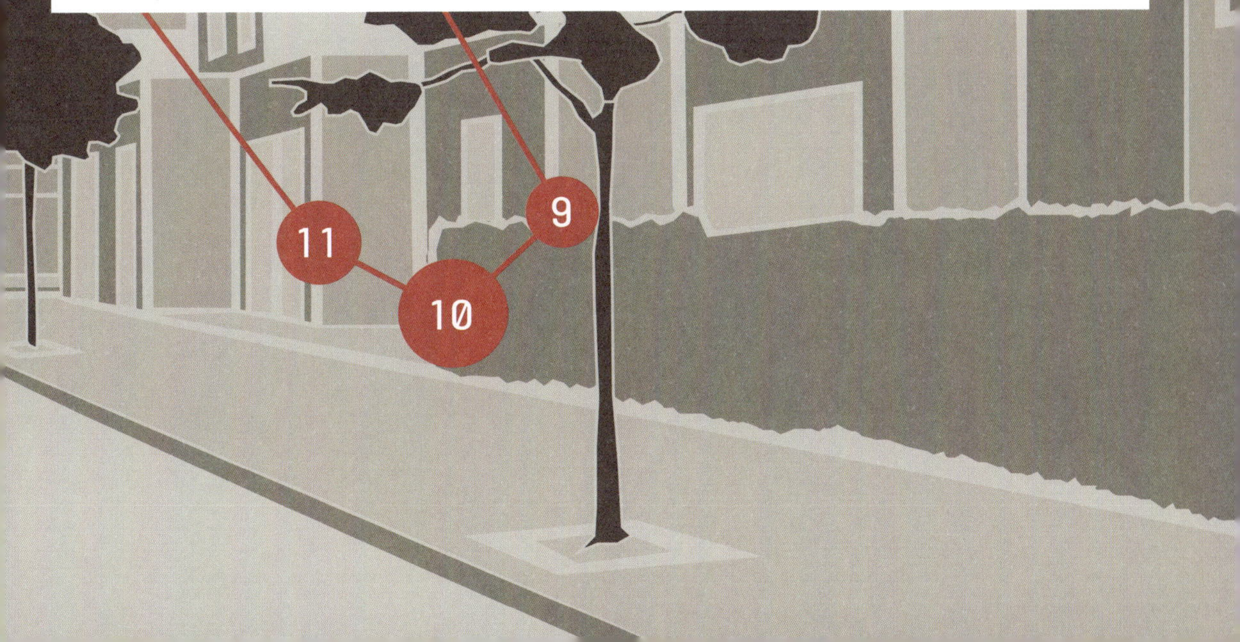

SELECTION OF AREAS AND STREETS

These twelve selected streets do not constitute a series, as in the famous *Great Cities* book by Alan Jacobs (1993). Nor do they possess the obvious historical layering of most of the examples used by Jan Gehl (2011) to highlight the importance of the space between buildings. What we present is a selection of streets that are more closely aligned with current practice and the densification challenge. That is why we opted for two types of streets that are most common in these kinds of areas: an access road with a wide street profile and generally speaking a lot of motorized traffic, and a street with a narrow profile and, usually, a focus on the pedestrian.

The issue here is how the applied design solutions in these two street types actually impact on the users, and to what extent these design solutions create a human scale. For the perspective we used Street-View images: taken from the centre of the street space with a good view of both street edges. Although pedestrians spend most of their time on the footpaths, they cross the street several times, which allows them to absorb the entire streetscape. The big advantage of this perspective is that it shows both sides of the street to the same degree - just as the design of the street space gives equal weight to both sides. What is more, it is a perspective that is nowadays just a mouse click away for nearly all urban spaces.

How do these places actually work in terms of physical structure and layout? Which particular solutions were employed and in what combinations?

FIG. 4.1 The Sensing Streetscapes consortium analysing the twelve streets from six different cities.

The six cities and twelve streets were subsequently systematically deconstructed and analysed according to the same research through design method and in collaboration with the consortium of spatial design experts [FIG. 4.1]. In our approach, research through design entails applying the insight of the spatial design professional to produce a systematic and revealing analysis of the different situations. It is not our objective to pass judgement in the sense of 'this is succeeding' or 'this is failing'. Our main aim is to transcend the level of anecdotal knowledge and subjective memory. Because what matters is how these places really work in terms of the physical structure, layout and effects on human experience. Which particular design solutions were applied, in what combinations? And what are the size and scale, especially in comparison with the other analysed streets?

EXPERT ANALYSIS AND USER EXPERIENCE

In his still relevant *To Scale* (2008), Eric Jenkins presented one hundred squares drawn to the same scale. The simplicity of the same scale and of the morphological imagery is basic but powerful. Jenkin's aim is equally clear: it creates a 'frame of reference' for the professionals' and students' design exercise, and at the same time immediately places the reference locations in the situational context. Another book that presents different cities in terms of identical sets of plans, sections, dimensions, programme and isometrics is Joan Busquets and Dingliang Yang's weighty *Urban Grids* (2108). Readers are able to study individual projects and then immediately compare them with other situations. We, too, have opted for this systematic approach and set-up.

In the graphic analyses we work with reduction and representation. In research through design the street space is reduced to the essential load-bearing structures and typical patterns. The focus of these analyses is on the impact on the user, and in particular on the design solutions that deliver a human scale for the user at street level in the given situations. Neuroarchitecture research is then employed to see how the structure of the street space affects user experience. This user experience of the street space was investigated in a series of neuroarchitecture tests involving thirty research participants [FIG. 4.2].

DATA VISUALIZATION WITH HEATMAPS AND GAZEPATHS

To produce the heatmaps the eye-movement patterns of all participants were superimposed. This revealed which elements of the street space attracted the most attention and how that attention was distributed across the space during the five seconds the image was visible. In the analyses we focus on the second to the fifth seconds on the assumption that these are the most important for capturing subconscious viewing behaviour. In the first two seconds people look only at the centre of the image.

FIG. 4.2 Test setup for this lab test.

These heatmaps are supplemented with analysis of the gaze-paths: the route followed by the eye and the differences in fixation duration between the elements people scan. Whether participants are positive or negative about the space is gauged by their response to the statement 'I would like to walk along this street', using a simple Likert scale of 1 to 5. After completion of the test the user experience is analysed per city, taking both streets together.

The selected streets with the chosen viewpoints provide a powerful perspective on these reference locations. It is from this perspective that the street is analysed. The cities are arranged in an order that gradually culminates in street spaces in which we can see that the design solutions for a human scale are most apparent.

VANCOUVER

WEST END

Vancouverism is a well-known term in high-rise. It stands for building tall but ensuring a soft landing on the street. Vancouverism is subject to a number of rules. High-rise and towers are designed as podium buildings: the high-rise stands on a base that aligns with eye level. In the surrounding streets there are still open spaces between the towers and buildings, which have a certain counterbalancing effect. Compared with other cities, extremely tall buildings and small-scale suburban development alternate easily in Vancouver and so too in the two model streets.

STUDY AREA

Area size	7.1 ha	**Tallest building**	201 m
High-rise construction year	1957-2008*	**Height/width ratio Area average**	1:2.1
Population density	22k inh/km^2**		
Distance from centre	0.4 km	**Selected streets**	Alberni Street West Giorgia Street
Ground Space Index	0.4		

* *It began in 1957 as the 22-storey Georgian Towers and is now being replaced by a 49-storey apartment tower. Trump Tower was completed in 1983 and Living Shangri-La in 2008.*

** *Population density of study area and surrounding streets.*

MORPHOLOGY

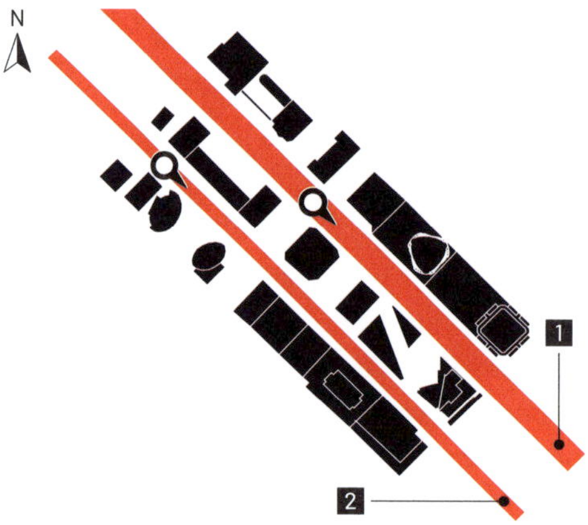

1 West Georgia Street
2 Alberni Street

Buildings
Viewpoint

BUILDING HEIGHTS

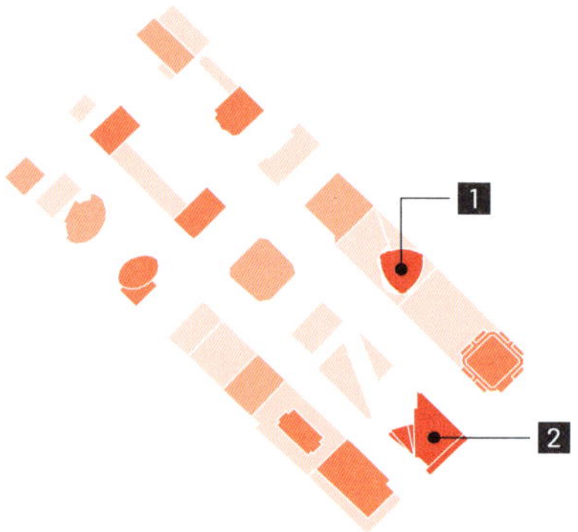

1 Trump Tower (188m)
2 Living Shangri-La (201m)

Very tall (150-300m)
Tall (80-150m)
Medium (30-80m)
Low (0-30m)

Vancouver, with 645,000 inhabitants, is Canada's third city. Located on the Burrard Inlet on the west coast in British Colombia, the city is wedged in between the wilderness of English Bay and Burrard Inlet in the north and the Fraser River in the south. The city of Vancouver came into being in the nineteenth century, acquiring its name and city status in 1886. Its development was given added momentum by the construction of the Canadian Pacific Railway (1881-1885). The renovated timber Abbott House on Georgia Street is one of the few surviving structures from that early period.

Like many North American cities, its street layout is based on the grid. In Vancouver this consists of elongated lots, the long sides running southeast-northwest and the short sides southwest-northeast. The infill of the lots is very diverse as the size and scale of the urban planning grid ranges from fine- to coarse-grained.

West End is part of Downtown Vancouver, the original urban core on the Burrard Peninsula. Owing to its location on a peninsula, Downtown Vancouver's grid lies at an angle of 45 degrees to the metropolitan grid and is structured by a number of access roads: Georgia Street, Robson Street and Davie Street in the long direction and Denman Street, Thurlow Street and Burrard Street in the short direction. Burrard Street and Georgia Street are by far the most important connections with the rest of the city.

The elevation map shows a cluster of high-rise in the middle of an area of mainly low to medium rise, and a few landmark buildings like Shangri-La and Trump Tower, which at 201 and 188 metres (659 and 616 feet) respectively are markedly taller. The area is characterized by its 'podium towers' in which the tauter and sterner high-rise section provides the keynote of the composition,

MIXED-USE

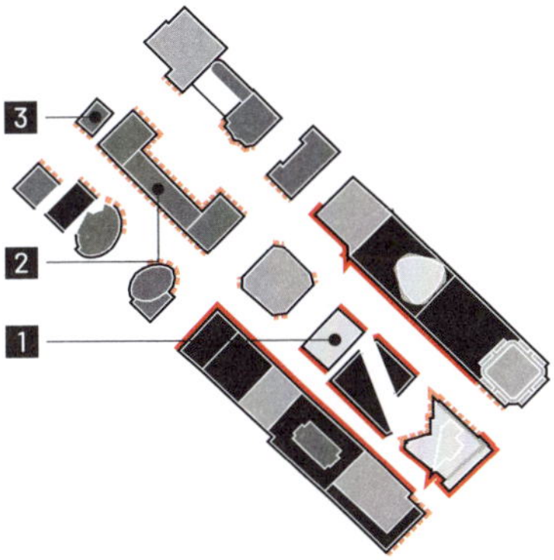

1 Coastal Church
2 Row houses
3 Abbot House

- Mix
- Housing
- Offices
- Other
- Closed GFL*
- Active GFL*
- Semi-active GFL*
- Unknown

* Ground Floor Level

CONNECTIVITY

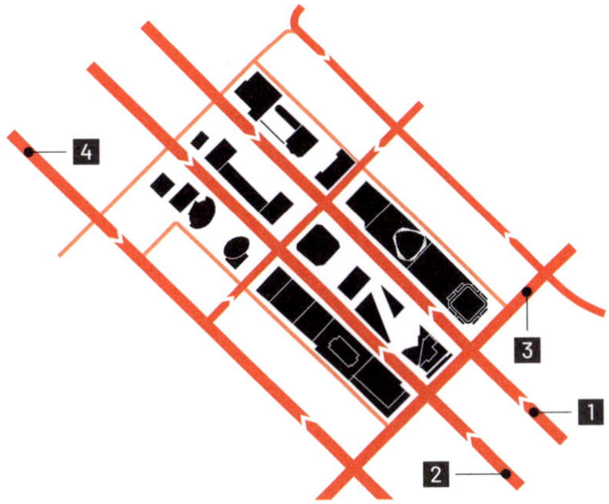

1 West Georgia Street
2 Alberni Street
3 Thurlow Street
4 Robson Street

- Main roads
- Side roads
- Railway/ Metro line

while the podiums offer a more fine-grained architectural expression and rhythm at eye level. In fact the podium height enables the application of multiple design solutions that determine the transition between public and private while also helping pedestrians on their way. High-rise is more indirectly part of the street. At a higher level of scale Vancouverism delivers a relatively open street plan.

West End borders Stanley Park and is primarily a residential area. Nevertheless, it has a rich mix of uses. There are high concentrations of shops and restaurants in the southeastern part around Robson Street, Davie Street and Denman Street. However, the study area around West Georgia Street is characterized by a higher density of offices and hotels whereas the southeastern part of the study area towards the city centre features an unbroken wall of active ground floors. Owing to its many shops and restaurants plus the parks and beaches on the southwest side, it is a popular destination.

West Georgia Street, which is one of the two selected streets in this area, is one of the most important thoroughfares in Downtown Vancouver. It runs along the boundary between West End and Coal Harbour, Vancouver's waterfront, which has the highest concentration of skyscrapers. Alberni Street, the other street in the study, lies two streets further south and runs parallel to West Georgia Street. It is more residential in character.

ALBERNI STREET

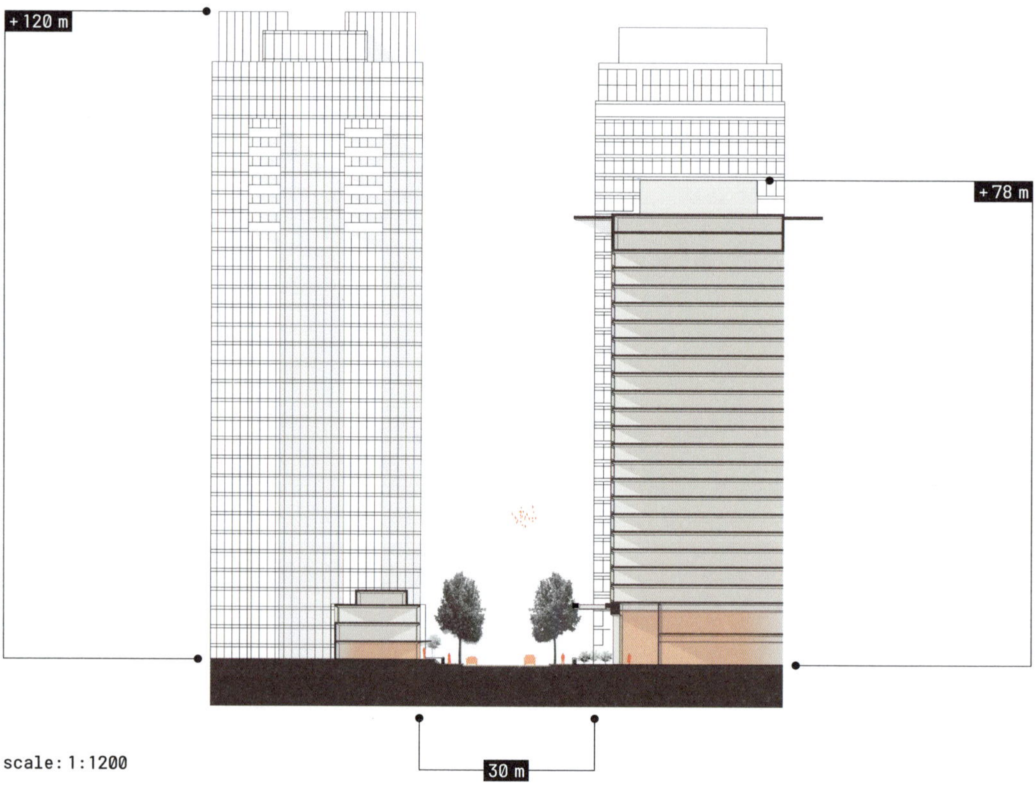

scale: 1:1200

ALBERNI STREET

The section of Alberni Street between Thurlow and Jervis Streets, which we have studied in terms of user experience, has a height-width ratio of 1:3.8 and is characterized by remarkable jumps in scale. This is clearly visible in the street profile, where apartment towers alternate with ground-accessed dwellings. The dwellings along the street have a simple transition zone consisting of a short flight of steps. On the apartment tower opposite an eight-metre-high awning above a series of window openings acts as a literal partition between the pedestrian and the high-rise. The design of the public space is similarly layered, with a street profile of trees interspersed with small-scale elements.

The Main Structure

On the northeast side of the street (left side in the images) the row houses are prominent as their ground and three upper floors define the street edge. The row is designed as a series of individual dwelling units with a fine-grained rhythm and a wealth of detailing. It is almost suburban. The row houses continue a bit further where the apartment building is set back and then proceed. The row houses have a complex massing made up of party walls, a cantilevered storey, a porch and stairs leading to raised terraces.

Although less detailed, the perforated awning of the apartment building serves to reduce the scale of the abstract, uniform volume towering above it. At pedestrian level the concrete awning forms a visual boundary. A set-back ground floor ensures that the cylindrical tower further down on the southwest side (right side in the images) does not dominate the footpath. The cantilevered section is supported by columns. The horizontal articulation of the mass of the apartment tower in the background on the northeast side renders it less monolithic.

Linked Contrasts

There is a stark contrast between the fine-grained row houses at street level and the austerely designed tower above. Like the row houses and the cylindrical tower opposite, this high-rise tower is horizontally articulated at ground floor level, but vertically articulated above.

At eye level the many concrete awnings reinforce the horizontality of the street and the connection between the buildings. It is such elements that succeed in softening the marked height and verticality. Sometimes literally – the awnings obscure the view of the towers above, even though they remain emphatically present in the form of a 'second layer'.

The street-level profile shows that, despite their differences in scale, the street edges are carefully aligned. The apartment tower awning is at much the same height as the roof of the row houses opposite, such that the tower and the ground-access dwellings combine to shape the street space. The street profile reveals how the design of the street manages the transition from public to private space.

DETAILS

1

3

2

4

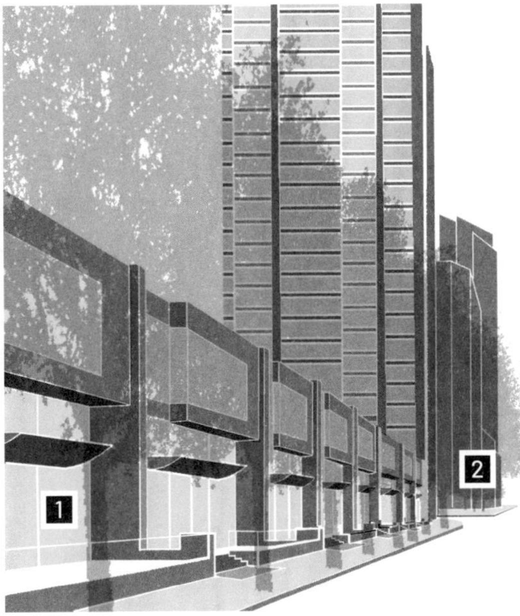

Fine-grained Transition

In the row houses an awning above the entrance, together with a low wall and hedge and steps, subtly marks the transition to the private indoor space of the dwelling. Property boundaries normally associated with a low-rise suburb, such as hedges and garden walls, contribute to the sense of a human scale here. The buildings themselves also reflect the use of various principles aimed at managing the transition from a large level of scale to that of the pedestrian.

Without denying the presence of high-rise, the pedestrian space in Alberni Street is primarily defined by small-scale, tangible elements in the public space. At eye level these elements deliver a layered transition between dwelling and street. The row of trees on either side of the street softens the view of the apartment towers and define the pedestrian zones vis-à-vis the relatively wide roadway. The parked cars on either side of the street are obtrusive but provide pedestrians with a further layer of protection from the traffic.

Hard Materials

The materials used in this section of Alberni Street consist for the most part of glass, concrete, metal and asphalt, predominantly in shades of grey. The front doors of the row houses are among the few elements that add a touch of colour to the street. Tactility is mainly to be found in the small-scale, green design of the public space, such as the rows of trees, and the planting of hedges along the property boundaries of the ground-accessed dwellings. The street has a green character that, in the growing season at least, partially compensates the colourlessness of the architecture.

BUILDING VOLUMES

GROUND FLOOR

STREET LEVEL

scale: 1:600

FORTIS BC

WEST GEORGIA STREET

scale: 1:1200

WEST GEORGIA STREET

Compared with Alberni Street, West Georgia Street looks and is more urban: the roadway has two extra lanes, the ground floors are more active, the buildings are taller and there are bus stops. As in Alberni Street shifts in scale are an important feature of the streetscape of West Georgia Street and the height-width ratio of 1:7 is more extreme. In profile Trump Tower and Shangri-La immediately stand out. They are two of Vancouver's tallest buildings and they form a stark contrast with the nearby Coastal Church from 1918. The church building is slightly set back, which actually lends it a certain grandeur in the midst of this high-rise world.

Minimal Scaling

The viewpoint is from the intersection with Bute Street. Unlike Alberni Street there is very little scaling of the building masses from the perspective of the pedestrian. The two buildings in the foreground act as 'wings' for the West Georgia Street 'street theatre'. The street edges have an interesting rhythm owing to the buildings and ground floors being set back from the property line. There are openings between the tall buildings. The entrance area is a few steps above the pedestrian space of the footpath, lending it a semi-public character.

Looking at the urban massing in West Georgia Street we see at eye level a varied layer of small-scale volumes, buildings and set-back ground floors. Above that, without much in the way of transition, is a second level of abstract, functional towers. The facade of the building in the foreground on the southwest side steps down to the lower level. That attempt to create a transition is only partially successful, despite the deep window reveals. The reveals (i.e. the inner surfaces of the material surrounding a window opening) affect the play of shadow and depth in the elevation.

Subtle Transitions

At eye level, the street edges in West Georgia Street display a wealth of architectural forms and design solutions. Above eye level the glazing and hard composition of the towers delivers a more functional uniformity.

A distinctive feature of the streetscape is the combination of set-back ground floors and a vertical articulation. This is very obvious in the building in the foreground on the northeast side (left side in the images) of the street. The ground floor has been opened up, creating public space, in combination with a commercial use on the building's ground floor.

Closed Buildings

Above ground floor height, and like Trump Tower, the building has a horizontal composition, whereas the Shangri-La tower in the background is characterized by a combination of vertical silhouette and horizontal facade structure. Trump Tower also has a set-back, transparent ground floor with a sloping roof supported on slender steel columns. The building on the southwest side of the street (right side in the

DETAILS

1

3

2

4

images) has deep window reveals combined with an emphatically vertical structure. One visual effect of the deep reveals is to make the building seem closed and inaccessible. Conversely, the various open ground floor sections along this street serve to strengthen both the sense of accessibility and the interaction between the street front and the internal world of the building.

The ground floor and awning height of Trump Tower are aligned with the Coastal Church opposite. In both cases the elevation is set back from the street and there is a difference in level compared with the ground plane. The few steps bridging the difference lend that area a semi-public character.

Brutalist

The architecture of the buildings in the foreground is brutalist: the building on the northeast side has a neutral facade while the building on the other side of the street has a strong three-dimensional facade thanks to deep window reveals. Trump Tower has a twisted, sculptural form and a glazed curtain wall. The rounded balconies on the corner lend the otherwise smooth tower a modicum of plasticity. Below the awning of Trump Tower stands a box-like volume with a shiny black cladding. The Coastal Church by contrast is a traditional building, brick-built with arched window openings and a shallow-pitched roof. Most of the other facades in West Georgia Street feature smooth materials and copious reflective glass.

The design of the public space is dominated by the six lanes of traffic. There is space for parallel parking along one side but most of the parking is catered to elsewhere. The pedestrian space is separated from car traffic by a row of trees and street furniture. The footpaths are finished in different types of paving. The use of tiles and the rectangular pattern in which they are laid help to reduce the wide street space to human dimensions. Remarkably, despite the wide street profile

BUILDING VOLUMES

GROUND FLOOR

STREET LEVEL

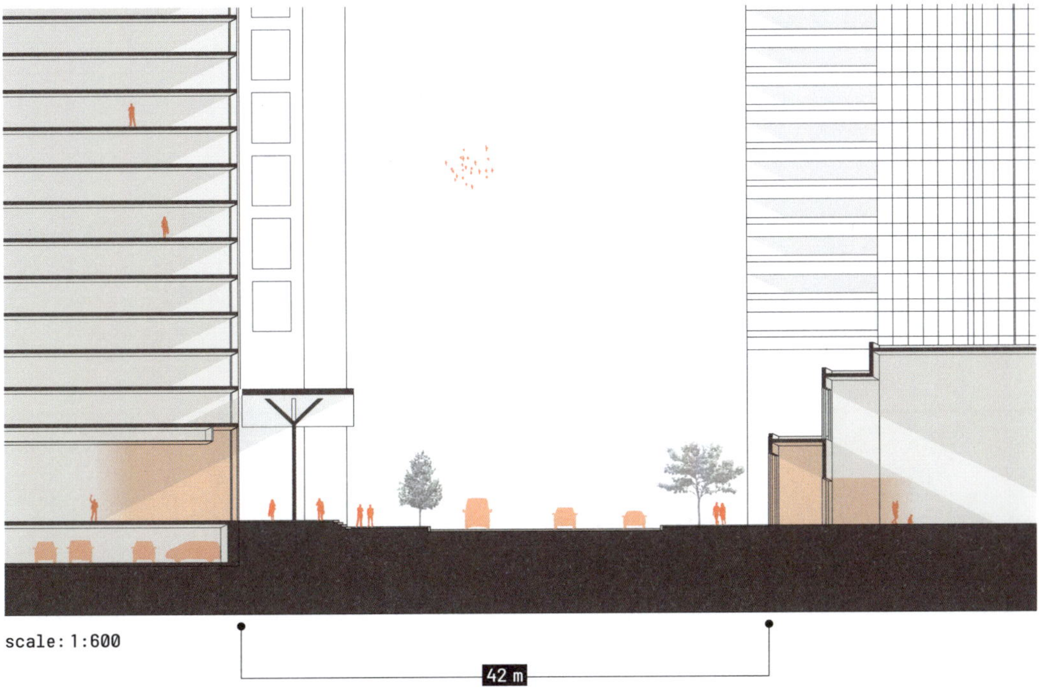

and relatively tall towers the planners opted for small trees that have a limited aesthetic effect. Perhaps they actually wanted to retain a view of the towers?

Human Scale?

Another question raised by the public space in West Georgia Street, is the level of scale deemed to represent the human scale. This street clearly has a function as a traffic artery. Opportunities for scaling to a human scale are limited. Because of the open urban structure in this part of Vancouver the only quasi sheltered spaces are behind and between the buildings. The question is to what extent they are able to counterbalance the intrusive street space of West Georgia Street. By extension, that question holds for all Vancouver. In a city located in the middle of a vast wilderness and imposing nature, perhaps a higher density and intense urbanism can be partly counterbalanced by the presence of nature outside the city? In large parts of the Dutch landscape there is no such conveniently nearby counterbalancing factor. What can designers do to take account of this in their design?

USER'S PERSPECTIVE

ALBERNI STREET

Despite very tall towers, a variety of design solutions are deployed in Vancouver's West End aimed at lending the street space a human scale. Different though they are, Alberni Street and West Georgia Street share some similarities, like the radical separation between tower and the set-back podium at eye level. These street-level podiums are variously detailed via subtle and fine-grained interventions. To see what effect this has on users we employed neuroarchitecture to systematically test a group of research participants (see Chapter 3 for an explanation).

In the more residential Alberni Street, the detailing is of a high order and that is reflected in the way people scan the street space. The eye patterns (see heatmap) are broadly distributed. On both the northeast and southwest sides attention was paid to elements at eye level, such as the front doors of low-rise buildings, trees, traffic furniture and the awnings. As we shall see in the neuroarchitecture tests for other streetscapes, parked cars automatically draw the eye. That is revealed by the gazepaths (see gazepath A), which map the route travelled by the eye in greater detail.

The design of the street makes it difficult to discern other people in a single glance, witness the relevant scanpath. The tall towers are seen, but visual attention focuses mainly on the ground floor zone, on elements like the awning (see gazepath C). The eye also settles on the passer-by who can be seen on the other side of

WEST GIORGIA STREET

the street between two parked cars. People also look at the greenery of the rows of trees on either side of the street and at the striking entrance to the foremost row house (see also gazepath B).

The user experience of West Georgia Street is quite different. In a reflection of its traffic function, the heatmap reveals that many traffic elements such as cars, traffic lights and signs attract a lot of attention (see gazepath D). This also generates long eye travel distances between individual fixation points, meaning that people look switch their gaze at an accelerated rate. This reaction is probably triggered by safety risks associated with traffic (see also information processing in Chapter 3). We also see that the brutalist building in which windows and doors are barely visible attracts almost no attention. But people do scan the trees and tall towers (see also gazepath E). Vertically, viewing behaviour is cut off by the roof of the church and the awning (see also gazepath F).

ALBERNI STREET

A Focus on parked cars and width of the street profile. High-rise also visible.

B Eyes focused on the entrance to the ground-level houses in sunlight.

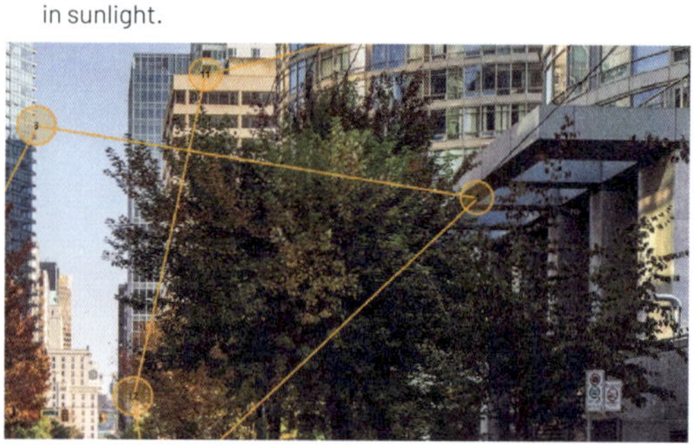

C Awning provides definition and direction.

WEST GIORGIA STREET

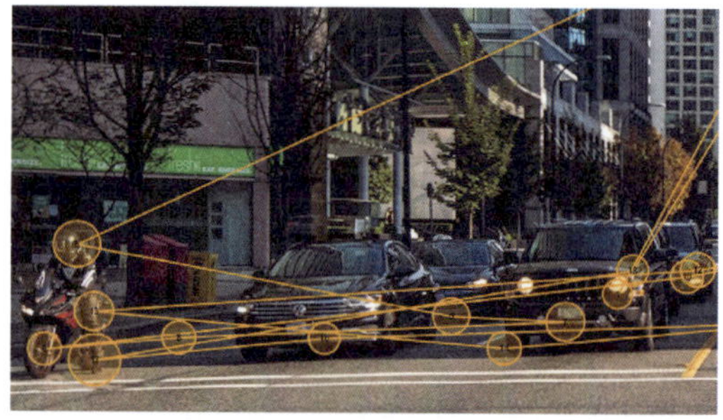

D Many fixations on oncoming traffic.

E High-rise also attracts attention.

F Focus on height of street level via awning and church.

CONCLUSION

The effect of typical examples of Vancouverism is clearly seen in the two West End streets studied. The podium building structure radically detaches the visual bulk of the austere towers from the building at eye level. The smaller-scale buildings also provide continuity in the street space, with the mass of larger buildings in the background.

In West Georgia Street visual variation is provided mainly by the large awnings and active ground floor with commercial uses, while in Alberni Street it takes the form of a soft, layered transition between street space and street edge, and between public and private space.

Generally speaking the solutions used in Alberni Street work to create a human scale at the level of the pedestrian, while the partial absence of such interventions in West Georgia Street results in a more tentative scanpath. This is confirmed by people's assessment of the streets. Out of all twelve streets, Alberni scored the highest rating from the participants in the neuroarchitecture test. West Georgia Street's rating stalled at 'neutral'.

In both streets the wide asphalted roadway tends to push the pedestrian zones visually to the edges of the street. This is further reinforced by the cars, either parked or waiting at traffic lights.

TORONTO

OLD TORONTO

Compared with the other cities in this study, Toronto's high-rise buildings land unapologetically right on the building line. This is certainly the case in Old Toronto. This is one of the most densely populated parts of the city and it also has the highest concentration of skyscrapers. Our user experience study in Toronto accordingly involves two of the more extreme street spaces.

Toronto, Canada' biggest city, is capital of the province of Ontario. Since its inception at the end of the eighteenth century the city has spread out along the shore of Lake Ontario. The Old Toronto district corresponds with the original city boundaries. Since the eighteenth century the city has expanded via incorporations and amalgamations with surrounding municipalities to its present size of around 2.93 million inhabitants. West End is part of Old Toronto and is bordered by King Street West, the most important east-west thoroughfare.

STUDY AREA

Area size	16.6 ha	**Tallest building**	261 m
High-rise construction year	1967-1990*	**Height/width ratio Area average**	1:5.1
Population density	8.2k inh/km²**		
Distance from centre	0 km	**Selected streets**	Wellington Street West Bay Street
Ground Space Index	0.6		

* *The TD Bank Tower opened in 1967 and in 1990 the area development was 'rounded off' with the construction of the Canada Trust Tower.*

** *Population density of all Old Toronto*

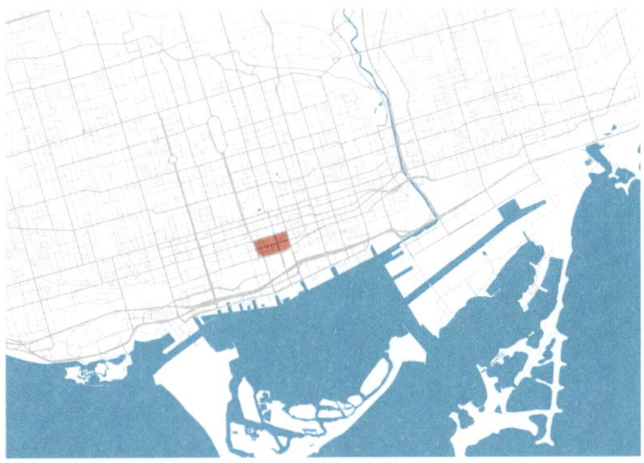

MORPHOLOGY

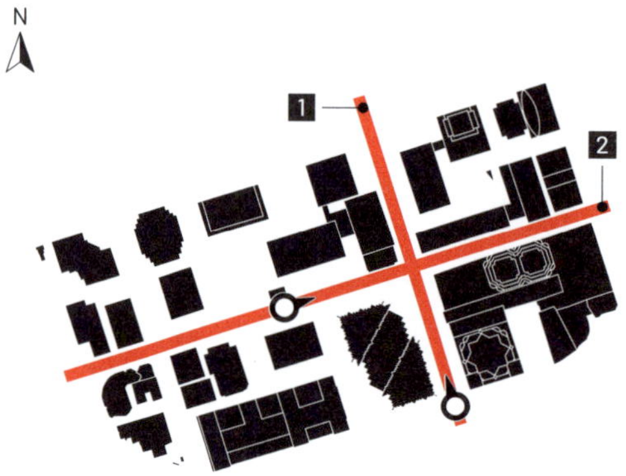

1 Bay Street
2 Wellington Street West

Buildings
Viewpoint

BUILDING HEIGHTS

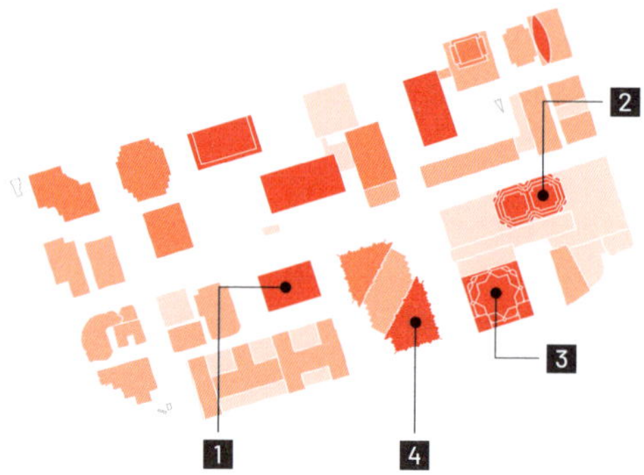

1 TD Bank Tower (223m)
2 Bay-Wellington Tower (207m)
3 TD Canada Trust Tower (261m)
4 Royal Bank South Tower (173m)

Very tall (150-300m)
Tall (80-150m)
Medium (30-80m)
Low (0-30m)

Like most North American cities, Toronto's urban plan is based on the grid, of which Old Toronto is the oldest part. In the east-west direction the grid is dominated by Wellington Street; in the north-east direction by York and Bay Streets, which are the most important traffic arteries in the city centre. Located on the south side of the area is Union Station, Toronto's main public transport hub.

On the morphological map the grid structure, dotted with large clusters of free-standing buildings and complexes, is clearly identifiable. The buildings are so large that together they form the street walls. But the map also shows a fair amount of public space. This contributes to a more open streetscape, something that is badly needed in an area dominated by massive high-rise.

The elevation map shows clusters of very tall buildings, among them the Bay-Wellington Tower (207 metres / 679 feet) and TD Canada Trust Tower (261 metres / 856 feet). Some towers are Toronto icons, like the 223-metre (731-foot) TD Bank Tower, part of Mies van der Rohe's Toronto Dominion Centre. Interspersed between the high-rise are low- and medium-rise buildings. A network of smaller streets provides access to the buildings and weaves them into the grid.

As far as the mix of uses is concerned, this area is dominated by offices, in particular financial institutions. Commercial services are tailored to this: more upmarket shops and a multitude of cafés and restaurants. The ground floors are generally semi-active. Active ground floors, usually consisting of restaurants and bars, can

MIXED-USE

1 Royal York Hotel
2 Toronto Dominion Complex
3 Allen Lambert Galleria

- Mix
- Housing
- Offices
- Other
- Closed GFL*
- Active GFL*
- Semi-active GFL*
- Unknown

* Ground Floor Level

CONNECTIVITY

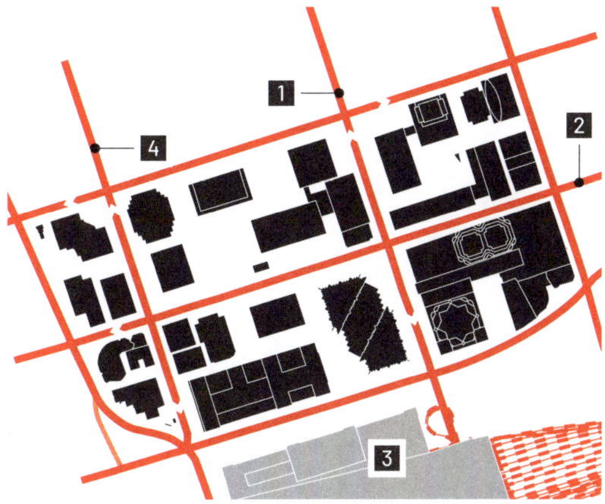

1 Bay Street
2 Wellington Street West
3 Union station
4 York Street

- Main roads
- Side roads
- Railway/ Metro line

be found on the southwest and southeast side (near Allen Lambert Galleria), close to the station. The area has few dwellings, but it does boast the huge Fairmont Royal York Hotel.

One of the selected streets is Wellington Street West. It begins in the west at Strachan Avenue and runs eastwards, changing into Front Street West after the intersection with Church Street. From the chosen viewpoint between two towers, the open character of the street is very evident. One characteristic of the street profile are the huge building complexes either side of a wide street space. Despite the width of the street, pedestrian space is limited. This is visually accentuated by the severe and marked verticality of the buildings, which have flat elevations and a high degree of repetition and abstraction.

Bay Street, the other street in the study, begins in the south at Queens Quay (Toronto's harbour) and ends in the north at Davenport Road. As in Wellington Street West, the chosen viewpoint is between two tall towers. The taller tower is TD Canada Trust Tower which is a staggering 261 metres (856 feet); the other tower is the 176-metre (577-foot) Royal Bank South Tower.

Bay Street is quite different from Wellington Street West. The Royal Bank South Tower has an indented elevation, and its lowest storeys are clad with reflective glass and dark materials. At street level the TD Canada Trust Tower stands on a six-storey podium and the street wall is interrupted by an arcade with the entrance to the Allen Lambert Galleria designed by Santiago Calatrava.

BEAUTY

WELLINGTON STREET WEST

+226 m
+155 m
54 m
scale: 1:1200

WELLINGTON STREET WEST

The street profile on both sides consists of a combination of very tall buildings and differences in level due to raised areas in the ground plane which, like the buildings themselves, are on the grand scale. The distances between the pedestrian space and the double-height ground floor are huge: 22 and 11 metres (72 and 36 feet) respectively. The street has four traffic lanes, but thanks to the street's 54 metre width the height-width ratio is a relatively modest 1:3.5.

Considerable Heights

The structure of the street space is chiefly determined by the sum of individual building complexes. Most volumes are rectangular, with a taut and functional termination, with the exception of the tower in the centre of the streetscape, which sports an octagonal crown. The elevations of the building complexes are also functionally expressed in a strong vertical composition. This emphasizes the height of the buildings, which are already pretty tall at 226 (741 feet) and 155 metres (508 feet). More than any other street in the study, the rhythm of this street space is determined by the succession of building volumes, aided by the staggered building lines of the individual buildings. The setback of buildings strengthens the monumentality of the street space.

Monumental Size

Various layers, connected by broad flights of steps, have been inserted between the private section in front of the building and the public section of the street. The resulting plateaus and colonnades impart a second, albeit subtler, rhythm to the street. The horizontal orientation of the imposing flights of steps provides a sense of direction and pedestrian space. The transitional zone between the private world of the building and the public outdoor space begins at the double-height ground floor vis-à-vis the main mass. That zone is terminated by a row of columns, followed by an entrance area that connects with the footpath via several platforms that are part of a wide flight of steps.

No Protection for Pedestrians

The actual pedestrian space is consequently geared to pedestrian through traffic, not to lingering. The pavements are narrow and wedged between the four-lane road and the encroaching flights of steps. The absence of a soft separation between traffic flows and the sparse street furniture offers scant protection or support for pedestrians.

At eye level there are virtually no design solutions aimed at achieving a human scale. The user is expected to conform to the building volumes and the message to pedestrians is not to get too close.

DETAILS

1

2

3

4

Hard Materials Dominate

Nor does the materialization offer much support. It is dominated by dark, smooth materials: steel, sheet materials and glass. The elevations in this part of the street are fairly flat and at most reveal a subtle plasticity in a play of lines visible only at close range.

Particularly notable is the two-metre (6 foot) blank wall that forms the hard border of the pedestrian space. The steps register because of their size rather than because of their materialization or detailing. The trees, instead of being aligned with the public space, are focused mainly on the facades. There is also some greenery in the residual spaces between buildings.

BUILDING VOLUMES

GROUND FLOOR

STREET LEVEL

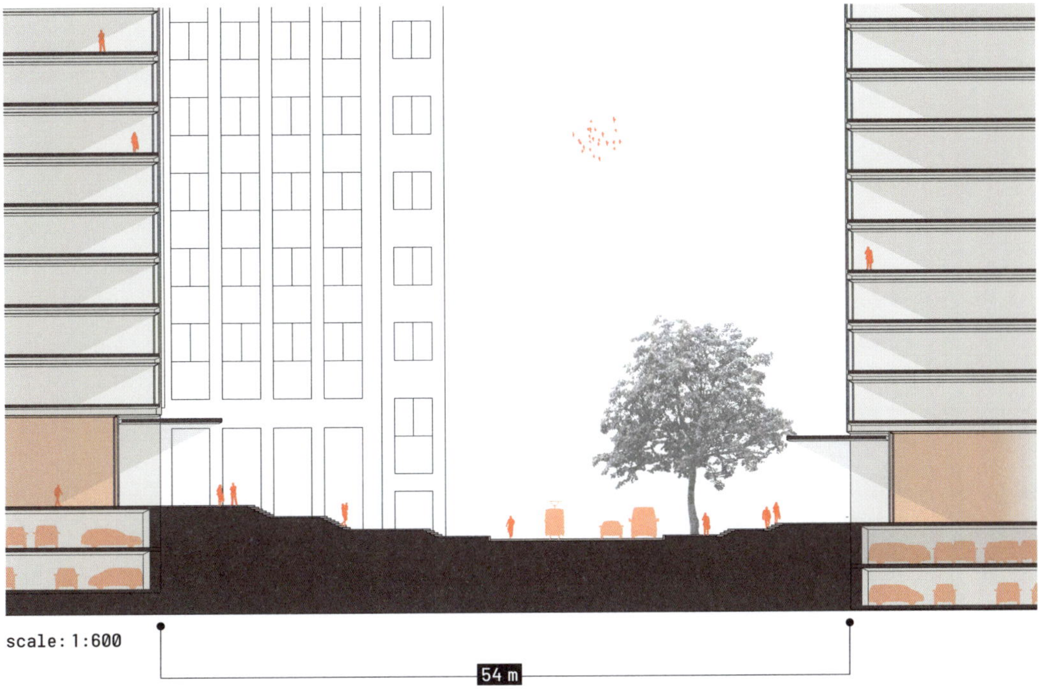

scale: 1:600

TD
CONNECT
RBC

BAY STREET

scale: 1:1200

BAY STREET

As in Wellington Street West the street space is defined by two very tall buildings. The height-width ratio is even more extreme: 1:6.3 compared with Wellington Street West's 1:3.5. The 261 metre (856 foot) TD Canada Trust Tower stands on a six-storey podium, so the street wall appears to be 24 metres (78 feet) high. Just visible at the end of the street is the tower of the Romanesque town hall. A major influence on the streetscape is the railway station, which is part of the street: the space allocated to pedestrian flows is considerably wider than in Wellington Street West.

Free-standing Building Masses

The Bay Street streetscape is determined by the variety of free-standing building masses that have sprung up within the gridded street pattern. The street space is defined by the variation in building lines. For example, beyond the indented building on the west side, the building line recedes, turning into a square-like space at the next side street. The buildings give space back to the street. Visually the setback building line opens up a view of the fronts of the buildings in the side street. This is fairly literally emphasized by the diagonal pattern of the footpath paving.

The east side seems lower because of the raised urban layer of the Trust Tower, which forms a continuous, four-and-a-half storey street wall. On the west side, the mass of the Royal Bank South Tower is indented and there are cantilevered sections from the fifth storey upwards. A dominant element in the street space is the clock tower of the Ontario court house, which the street meets at right angles.

Hard Landing

The Royal Bank South Tower on the west side (left side of the images) lands unmediated on the ground plane, although the lower storeys are embellished with a variation on the indented frontage. Clad with reflective glass and dark materials it comes across as impenetrable. On the corner is a display window advertising a clothing store elsewhere in the building. The east side of the street contains more design solutions aimed at the pedestrian. In addition to the tower setbacks and the 24-metre (78 foot) street wall with transparent ground floor, there is the striking steel structure of the entrance to the Allen Lambert Galleria. The tall, transparent ground floor is set back from the building line so that part of the pedestrian space is covered. The columns cadence the 24-metre (78 foot) street frontage.

On the west side, at ground level, the public pedestrian space on the corner of a side street is enlarged by a receding building line. This, together with the building behind, it lends the street space depth and rhythm, as do the differences in height, materialization and the use of setbacks.

DETAILS

1

2

3

4

Feels Inaccesible

In terms of design solutions, the difference between the east and west side of Bay Street is marked. The east side (right side in the images) has a decidedly horizontal articulation compared with the west side where the building complexes have an overriding vertical articulation. This difference applies to both the street front and the high-rise sections above. A noticeable feature of the streetscape are the flat elevations of the buildings in the foreground and the consequent lack of plasticity. The west side, with its reflective glass, makes a somewhat impenetrable impression. The ground floors in the streetscape are predominantly semi-active. In the foreground they consist of a combination of step landscape, platform and the space beneath the building's columns. The east side is quite different. The TD Canada Trust Tower, the tallest skyscraper in this area, is set back from the street, resulting in a four-and-a-half storey street wall.

Expansive Public Space

The lack of plasticity is not confined to the architecture, but is also evident in the expansive public space, which is all but devoid of detailing or refinement. A short row of trees flanks the pedestrian space on the east side of the street. The refined, slender steel structure of the entrance to the Allen Lambert Galleria really stands out in this fairly unsubtle environment.

BUILDING VOLUMES

GROUND FLOOR

STREET LEVEL

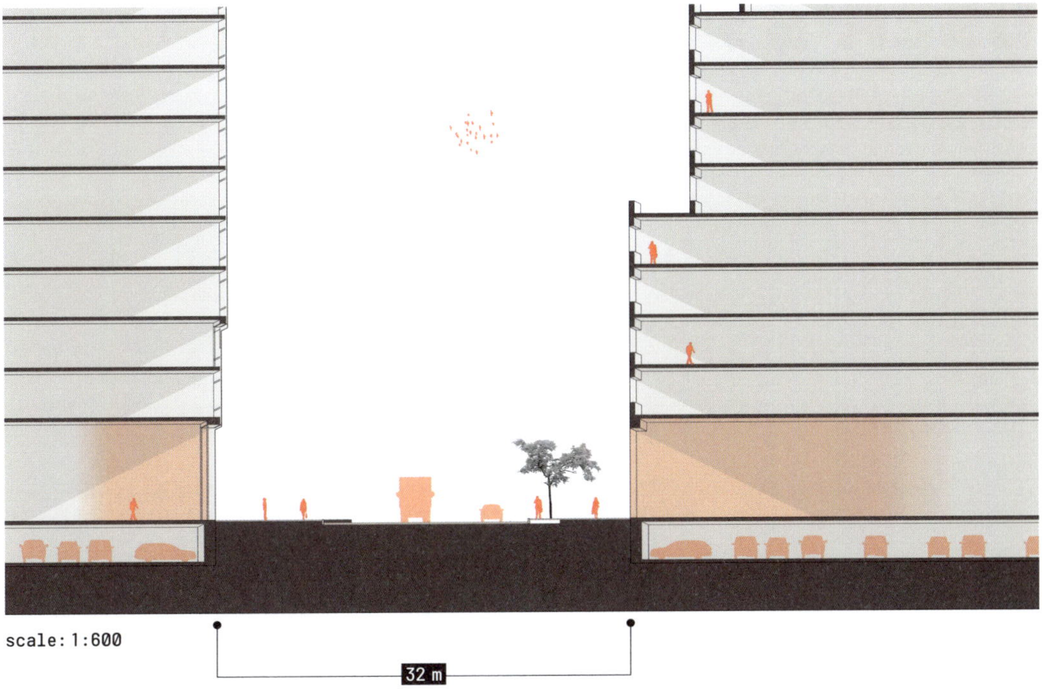

USER'S PERSPECTIVE

WELLINGTON STREET WEST

As in Alberni Street and West Georgia Street in Vancouver, there are big differences in the configuration of building volumes and street space and in how the buildings address the street space. Wellington Street West offers users of the street space very little in the way of a human scale. At least, not in the way this is spoken about now in architecture and urban design. The question is whether and how this makes itself felt in the visual experience. In both streets the heatmaps based on the aggregated viewing behaviour of thirty participants reveal a significant visual concentration on cars.

In Wellington Street West the staggered building lines ensure that buildings enter the visual field and attract attention. On the south side the illuminated part of the deep-set and raised ground floor plays a greater role, as do the reflections of buildings (see gazepath A) in the upper floors of the glazed tower. On the north side the gaze stops at the relatively lower front section of the high-rise. By contrast, the ground floor and the entrance areas of the two buildings attract scant attention. They are partially hidden from view or are dark because they are angled inwards.

The participants' gazepaths draw attention to the considerable width of street space that the eye has to span. The foreground of Wellington Street West seems to consist for the most part of asphalt and the darkness of the nearby ground floors attracts very little attention. In comparison with other streets in this study, there are hardly any places where you see or might expect to see people. Several gazepaths consequently show a

BAY STREET

rapid scanning pattern - especially with regard to the buildings closer to the street and in the distance (see also gazepath B). In a certain sense this viewing behaviour reflects the appeal of an urban layer or double-height ground floor (see gazepath C). The scanpath also reflects the more continuous linear suggestion of this space. The lack of human scale in the foreground offers little in the way of visual appeal or points of reference.

In Bay Street the participants' attention was attracted more to the whole width of the street space, thanks in large part to the rhythm in the street. On the west side the staggered building line served to bring the adjacent building into the visual field. The clock tower at the end of the street attracted a lot of attention and as such functions as a landmark (see gazepath D). On the west side reflections in the hard, indented building with coloured glass and the plethora of elements in the street space such as signs, flags and light poles, trigger scanning behaviour and long distances between fixations (see gazepath E). On the east side the Arcade serves to guide the gaze (see gazepath F). Finally, even the cars on the roadway attracted attention.

WELLINGTON STREET WEST

A Fixation on reflections on buildings and sun reflections.

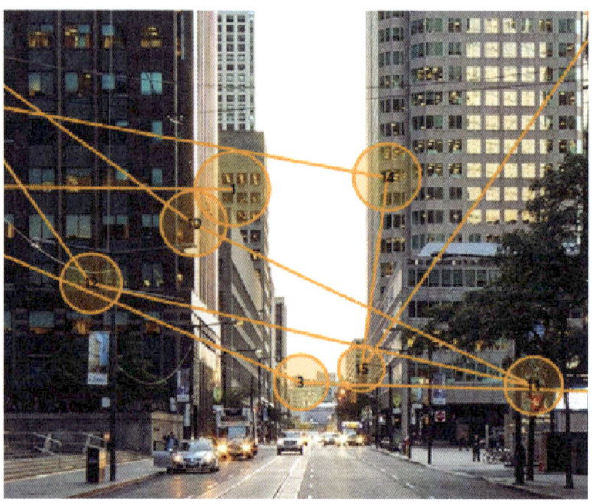

B Buildings brought into view by the staggered building line attract attention.

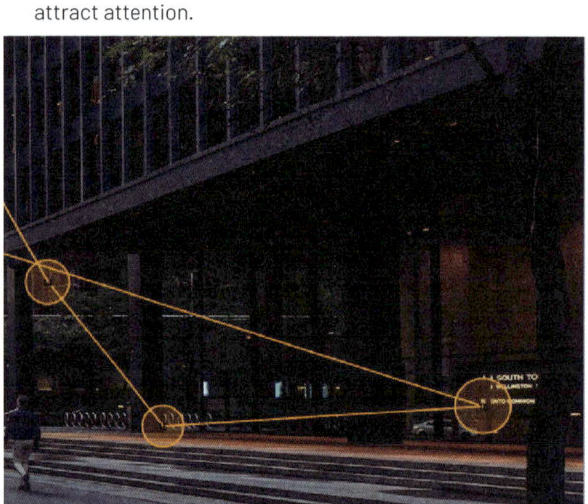

C It is mainly the illuminated part of deep-set ground floor that is seen.

BAY STREET

D The tower in the distance is noticed.

E Attention to streetscape elements like signs, flags and light poles.

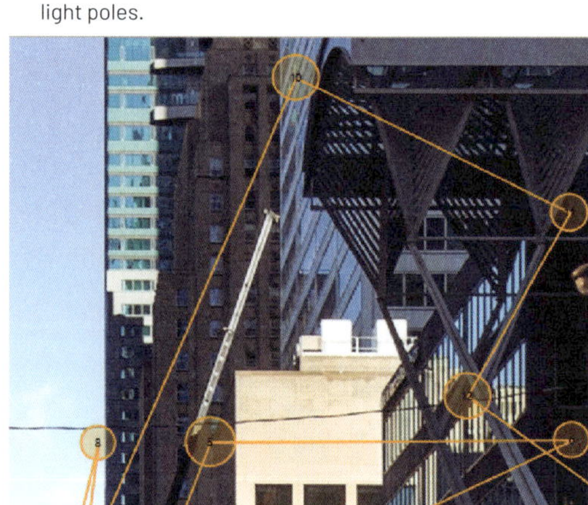

F The eyes fixate on the contours of the arcade.

CONCLUSION

Looking at the two streets in the Old Toronto study area we find that in Bay Street, compared with Wellington Street West, various design solutions aimed at introducing a human scale have been applied to the street space: the urban layer, raised ground floor, variety of building heights and the staggered building line.

The pedestrian flow from the station along Bay Street is a key feature and this finds expression in the arcade on the east side and the flattened corner on the west side, which creates a bit more open space. Because Bay Street is traffic artery for Toronto and the nearby station, a lot of space is reserved for traffic and the car, although parking is catered to elsewhere so that the street space is not (permanently) dominated by car traffic.

In Wellington Street West the high-rise meets the ground plane without any mediation, interruption or differentiation. What little differentiation there is on the ground floor and in the public space seems to be aimed more at making the public space part of the private world of the building rather than at establishing a connection with passers-by and other users. The negative impact of the concrete blank wall is amplified by the rather miserly space for pedestrians compared with that allocated to the car and to the semi-private space of the buildings. Pedestrians are not protected from the traffic.

Whereas Bay Street earned no more than a neutral rating from the neuroarchitecture test participants, Wellington Street West ranked fourth out of all twelve streets when participants were asked to rate the street on a scale of 1 to 5. The quality of the architecture (Mies van der Rohe) and the almost archetypical North American urban form of a street of high-rise buildings may explain why it scored slightly better than Bay Street.

Spinningfields

MANCHESTER

SPINNINGFIELDS

Manchester has a long history of high-rise. After a dip at the end of the twentieth century, the beginning of the new millennium saw renewed interest in the construction of unprecedentedly tall towers. Close to the Deansgate Square high-rise district, which boasts Manchester's tallest tower (201 metres / 659 feet), lies the modest densification location of Spinningfields. Unlike the other streets in this study, the two Spinningfields streets are largely car-free. In addition, a variety of means have been employed to tailor the street space to pedestrians, albeit with mixed results.

STUDY AREA

Area size	11.7 ha	**Tallest building**	92 m
High-rise construction year	1997-2017*	**Height/width ratio Area average**	1:2.4
Population density	3.9k inh/km^2		
Distance from centre	0 km	**Selected streets**	Hardman Street Atkinson Street
Ground Space Index	0.5		

* *In 1997 a developer started things off by purchasing the existing buildings and the plan to turn the area into a business district. The most recently completed building is the XYZ office building from 2017.*

MORPHOLOGY

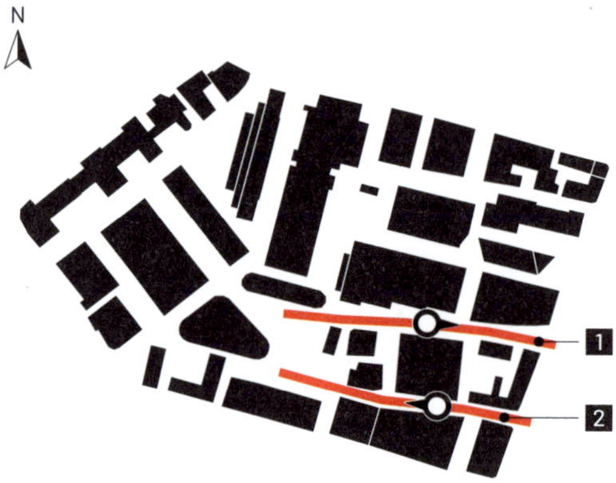

1 Hardman Street
2 Atkinson Street

Buildings
Viewpoint

BUILDING HEIGHTS

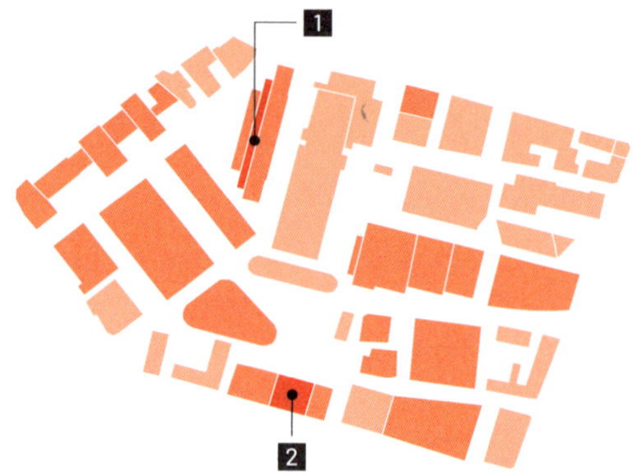

1 Civil Justice Center (80m)
2 No.1 Spinningfields (92m)

Tall (80-150m)
Medium (30-80m)
Low (0-30m)

Manchester, whose history dates back to the Roman period, is Great Britain's fourth city with a population of some 550,000. After centuries of being a medium-size town, the industrial revolution brought rapid growth. In Manchester, as in other cities, growth went hand in hand with the emergence of slums. Spinningfields, located in the city centre on the River Irwell, was one of them. Many of the slums here were demolished at the end of the nineteenth century but the district remained a deprived part of the Manchester. The initiative to redevelop Spinningfields came in 1997 and that plan was realized in the first decade of the twenty-first century. Today, there are always various small projects in development.

Spinningfields is a mixed area bounded by three major roads but is itself largely car-free. The roads to the north and south of the district - Bridge Street and Quay Street - connect Spinningfields with the area of the city on the other side of the River Irwell. Despite its compact size (some twenty buildings), Spinningfields boasts a network of public squares, boulevards and streets and a rich mix of uses with a total of 430,000 square metres of hospitality, commercial, residential and retail space. It also hosts the Manchester Crown Court, Manchester City Magistrates' Court and the Manchester Civil Justice Centre as well as several cultural facilities including a library, opera house, educational institutions and, in the northwest corner, the People's History Museum. Housing is concentrated along the riverbank and in the (partly historical) development on the north side of the district.

The functional mix is reflected in the size of the buildings. The area consists for the most part of medium-rise buildings with a few outliers like No. 1 Spinningfields (92 metres / 301 feet) and the Civil Justice Centre (80 metres / 262 feet).

MIXED-USE

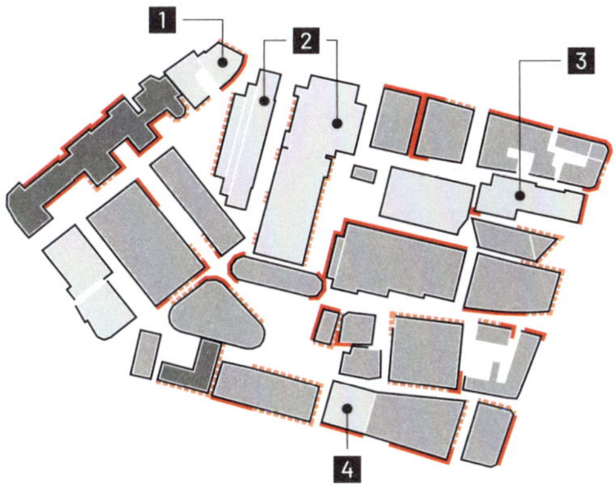

1 Peoples History Museum
2 New Magistrates' & Crown Courts
3 John Rylands Library
4 Sunlight House

Mix
Housing
Offices
Other
Closed GFL*
Active GFL*
Semi-active GFL*
Unknown

* Ground Floor Level

CONNECTIVITY

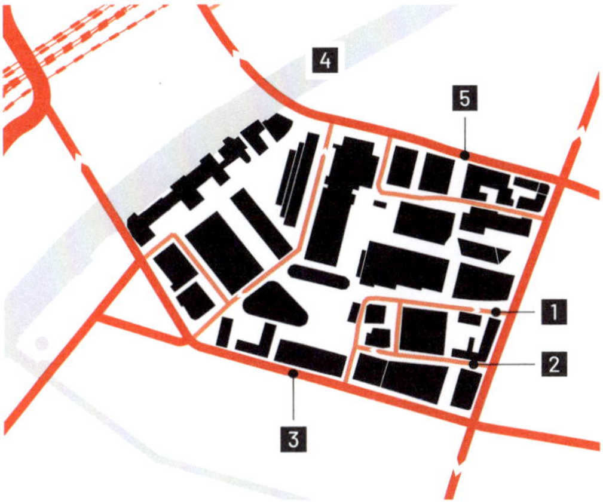

1 Hardman Street
2 Atkinson Street
3 Quay Street
4 River Irwell
5 Bridge Street

Main roads
Side roads
Railway/ Metro line

Prestigious buildings like John Rylands Building, Manchester Civil Justice Centre, Manchester Opera House, the People's History Museum and 'Northern England's first skyscraper', Sunlight House, are attractively designed and act as landmarks in the area.

The two streets in the study are Hardman Street and Atkinson Street. They are parallel but very different roads in the eastern part of Spinningfields. They run from Deansgate to Hardman Square. Hardman Street is crucial to the accessibility of the centre of Spinningfields while Atkinson Street is a narrow, one-way secondary street.

isg
isg
Hardman Street
Spinningfields

HARDMAN STREET

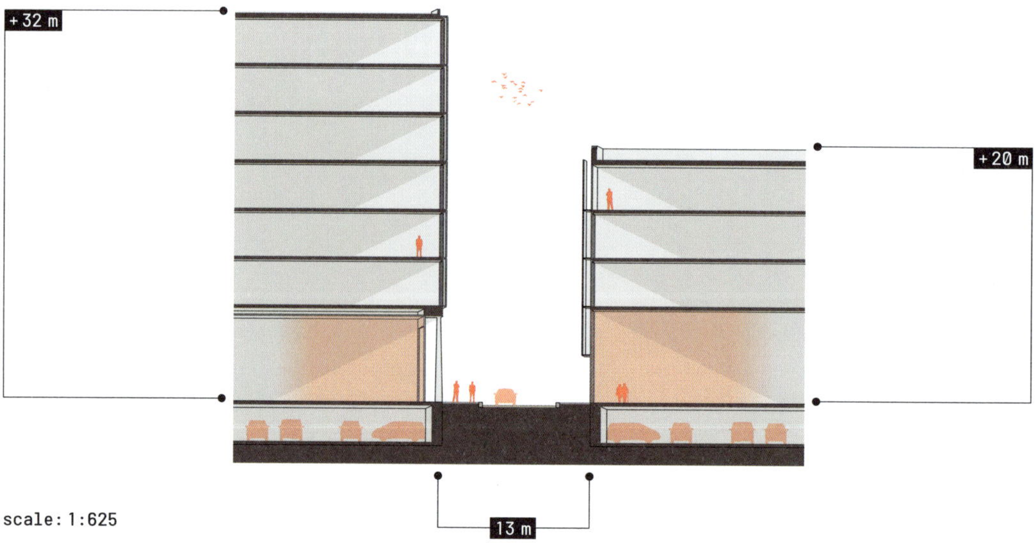

scale: 1:625

HARDMAN STREET

The height-width ratio of Hardman Street is 1:2. Compared with the streets discussed so far, the street profile is characterized by relatively low building volumes in relation to the width of the street. The north side of Hardman Street is formed by of a transparent building that rises from six to nine storeys. The two-storey base is set back, and the overhanging section is supported by four Y-shaped columns that define the streetscape. On the south side the frontages are more transparent and topped by glazed elevations which have a somewhat hermetic appearance thanks to a second skin of perforated metal sheeting on one of the buildings.

Traditional Urban Dimensions

In Hardman Street the urban mass consists of volumes that correspond to the street pattern. The volumes harmonize in both height and width with the traditional urban dimensions in nearby historical Manchester. Instead of toeing the building line, the buildings have been tailored to pedestrians with a variety of design solutions, including a set-back ground floor differentiated with awnings and transparent materials.

The street space is flanked by flat street walls with a lot of glazing. The public space in between is laid out as a pedestrian zone, including traditional paving. On the north side (left side in the images) the set-back ground floor allows more room for pedestrians. The pedestrian space is flanked by a modest row of trees that provides rhythm to the streetscape and creates a boundary between the footpath and the roadway. In addition, the pedestrian zones are defined by an extra wide kerb, which increases the pedestrian's sense of safety. Large dark grey planters placed on the building line lend the street frontage visual continuity.

Contact Between Indoors and Outdoors

Fully glazed curtain walls dominate this section of Hardman Street. The glass panels at ground level are predominantly horizontal, allowing pedestrians time to make contact with the interiors as they pass, whereas above the ground floor the glass panels are vertical, pointing to the sky. Various elements invest the public space with rhythm and articulation, such as the Y-shaped columns, bollards protecting the corner from the roadway, lines in the paving of the pedestrian space as well as the planters and the row of trees.

Despite the similarly transparent facades of three of the buildings on Hardman Street the effect at street level is very different. This is related to accessibility. The double-height base of the building on the north side, which contains hospitality functions, is active because it is both visually and physically accessible. The windows of the ground floor of the building in the background on the south side (right side in the images) are largely screened with privacy film; it contains the offices of a media company. While the multi-tenanted building in the foreground on the south side has a semi-active ground floor, both of these buildings are clearly less accessible.

DETAILS

1

3

2

4

Staggered Ground Floors

The ground floors of the buildings on Hardman Street have been differentiated vis-à-vis the upper storeys and on the north side the double-height ground floor is set back. The pedestrian space on the north side is wider and flanked by a short row of trees. The frontages along Hardman Street vary in height from one to several storeys. The setback of part of the street frontage generates a transitional zone between the building and the public space. Architectural elements like a glazed awning, a revolving door and Y-shaped columns increase the interaction between building and public space.

Subtle Smoothness

Glass and metal are the main materials used in this section of Hardman Street. Most of the elevations are flat and taut. Although vast areas of smooth, glazed facades carry a risk of sterility, that is not the case on Hardman Street where an effort has clearly been made to avoid this with meticulous and occasionally refined detailing. In the case of overhangs, the design of the awning soffits, the supports and the points where they meet is of crucial importance. The glazed awning, the modest overhang and the revolving door are all part of a rounded glazed corner. The trees and paving material provide tactility and improve the quality of the street space. Together with the planters they lend the space a sense of intimacy in the midst of some very big buildings.

BUILDING VOLUMES

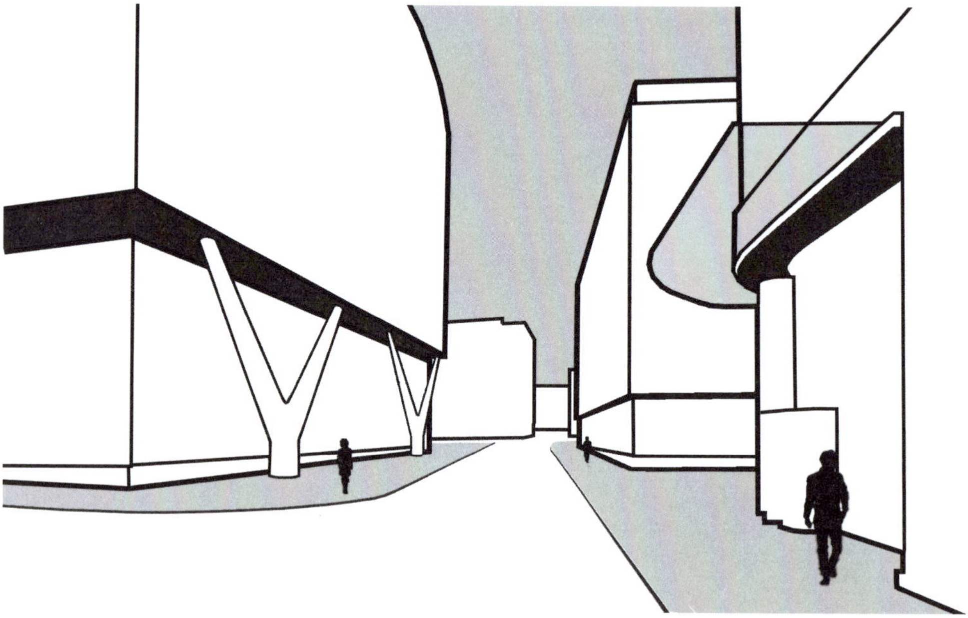

GROUND FLOOR

STREET LEVEL

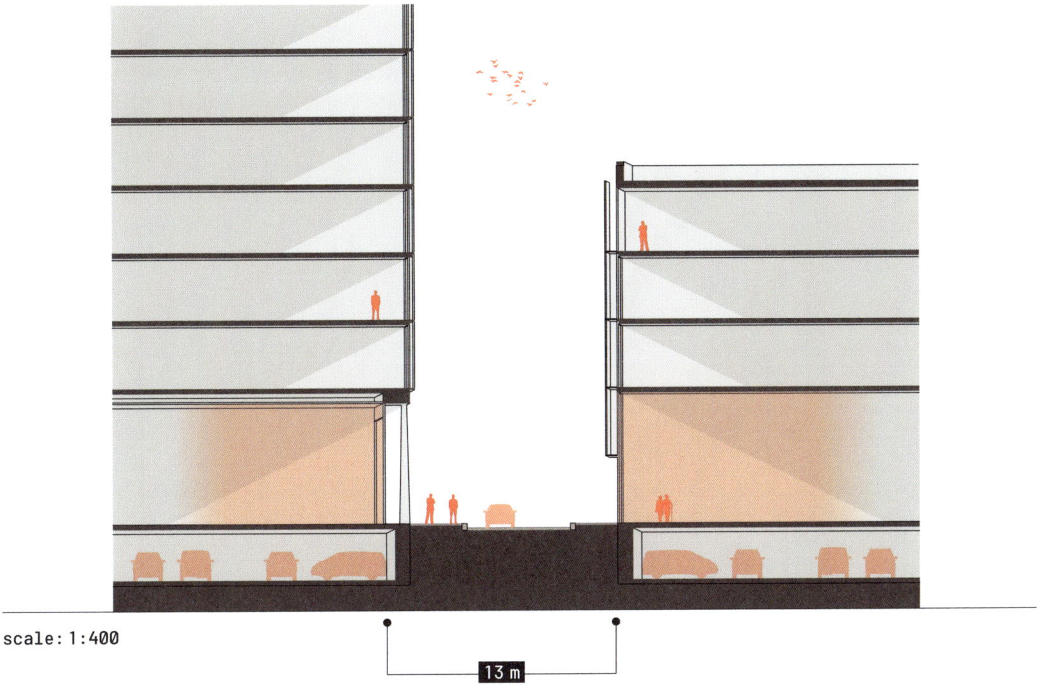

scale: 1:400

KEEP CLEAR
PARKING
FIRE EXIT

ATKINSON STREET

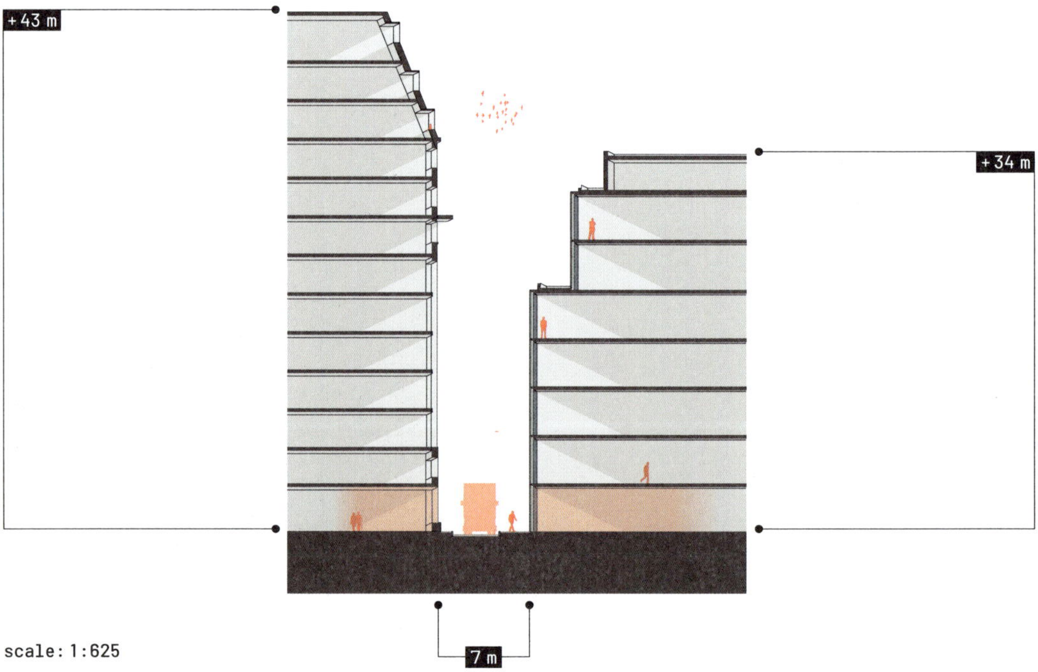

scale: 1:625

ATKINSON STREET

With its seven-metre-wide street profile, Atkinson Street looks more like the little streets in historical European cities than a street in a new-build area. Owing to heights ranging from 34 to 43 metres (111 to 141 feet), the height-width ratio (1:5.5) is almost as extreme as that of Bay Street in Old Toronto. The public space in Atkinson Street consists of a very narrow footpath on the south side (left side in the images), a one-way road, and a slightly wider footpath on the north side (right side in the images). Historical Sunlight House and the transparent office building on the other side of the street provide contrast in the streetscape. The two very different building volumes lend the street an organic character.

Cramped Street

Sunlight House, designed in 1932 by Joseph Sunlight, has fourteen storeys of which the top four are housed in a steep mansard roof. In the more recent, nine-storey building on the north side, whose top two storeys contain the mechanical services, a series of setbacks have been used to bring more light, air and space into the narrow street space.

Strong Contrasts

Built in the art deco style, Sunlight House is richly decorated and very sculptural. Conversely, the street edge opposite features a modern glass facade: flat, abstract and transparent. Yet the architecture of this building seems keen to engage with its older counterpart. Distinctive horizontal bands give the lowest two storeys a similar articulation to that of Sunlight House. What defines the street, apart from its narrow profile, is the gentle curve at the end, whereby both street walls appear to converge. This visual impression is reinforced by horizontal articulation of the buildings, bands, ground floor, staggered building lines and lines in the road surface.

Role of Detailing

In Sunlight House there is a subtle play with the detailing of the window and door frames and front doors which either recede or protrude, creating the suggestion of a facade divided into individual units. The facade opposite does almost the reverse. Here the marked horizontal articulation by means of bands and the greater transparency and lack of detailing and decoration makes fewer concessions to the human scale of the pedestrian. In addition, this facade is less expressive than that of Sunlight House where the framed openings, the ground floor street front and the positioning of the frames in the upper storeys all make for a high degree of plasticity.

The ground floors are flush with the edges of the narrow street space and are visually stretched to two storeys by means of a horizontal band. Only the modern transparent ground floor housing a restaurant is active. This is because the ground floor of Sunlight House currently functions as the rear of the building (the windows have been sealed and street access is elsewhere) and is therefore non-active. The same applies to the

DETAILS

1

3

2

4

car park entrance/exit further along the street. The fact that it is architecturally distinctive does not make it active.

Subtle Details

With the exception of the street lighting, the street space has no particular design in the form of street furniture or trees. It is too narrow for that. The front doors and their frames act as 'intermediaries' between street edge and street space. Nevertheless, some thought has been given to the design of the transition from building to public space and vice versa, using subtle details like doorsteps, a set-back frontage, a balcony with a slight overhang. The set-back ground floor of building in the background does deliver a transitional space that in this case has been used for a car park entrance/exit.

The facade of Sunlight House is highly detailed. It has plasticity in combination with a plethora of artisanal details, such as the many-layered arched lintel in Portland stone, the profiled and decorated frames and above that, the similarly decorated balcony. The overhang of the building in the background with the set-back ground floor rests on slender concrete columns. The abstract elevation in the foreground on the north side has a profiled aluminium band.

BUILDING VOLUMES

GROUND FLOOR

STREET LEVEL

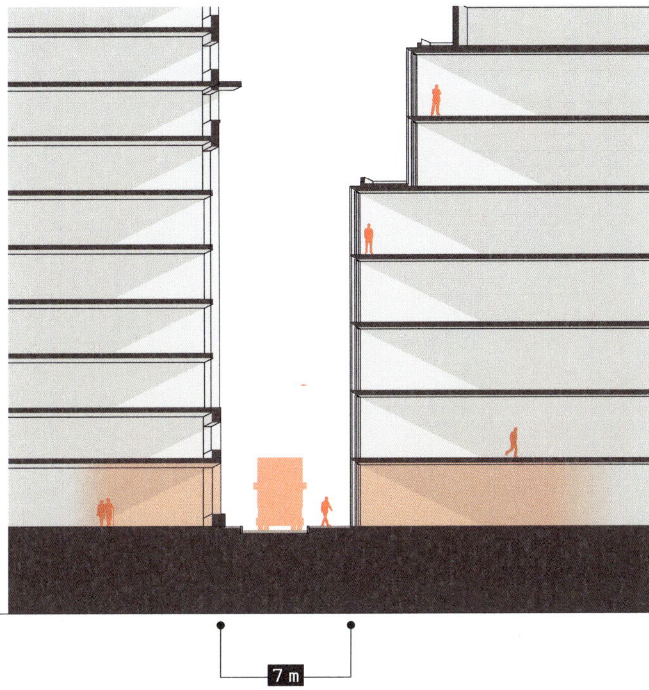

scale: 1:400

USER'S PERSPECTIVE

HARDMAN STREET

In both streets a variety of design solutions have been used to help reduce the visual massiveness to a human scale. The ground floors are active, but directly border the street space. Compared with street spaces where active frontages are hidden beneath deep overhangs, here they are clearly visible. The heatmaps reveal that eye level dominates the participants' experience, although there are big differences in fixation points and scanpaths.

The Atkinson Street gazepaths exhibit a central, circular scanning pattern. Quite a lot of attention is paid to the end of the street where the taller buildings stand. Within the narrow street profile the eye is drawn there via a slight curve in combination with the horizontal articulation of the facades. The staggered building line also plays a role, as demonstrated by the gazepaths (see gazepath A). For example, the building line juts forward so that the building in the background attracts attention.

The transparent glazed street front sometimes attracts very fleeting attention (see gazepath B) and then the participants' eyes are quickly drawn to Sunlight House. This also applies at ground floor level: rather than scanning the transparent glazed frontage of the more modern building, Sunlight House is scanned in detail, from the balcony to the windows on this storey (see gazepath C).

The Hardman Street gazepath exhibits a broad scanning pattern taking in the entire street profile. Apart from a wider street profile, the

ATKINSON STREET

overhanging building plays an important role. It leads the eye upwards via the Y-shaped columns, after which the eye travels to the other side of the street (see gazepath D), resulting in a higher visual field. In Hardman Street the facade on the south side, with its second skin of perforated metal sheeting, also attracts the eye, and after that the smooth glazed frontage below as it travels on to the entrance of the neighbouring building (see gazepath E).

ATKINSON STREET

A Set-back building line lends the perspective greater breadth and depth.

B In the narrow street attention bounces rapidly between both sides.

C The eye-catcher balcony draws attention to the second floor of the building.

HARDMAN STREET

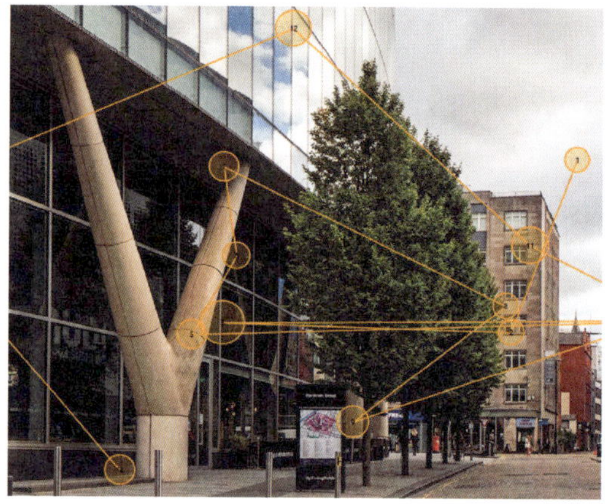

D The eye is led upwards via Y-shaped columns. Reflective material attracts relatively little attention.

E The planters lead the eye to the entrance while the functional facade materials attract little attention.

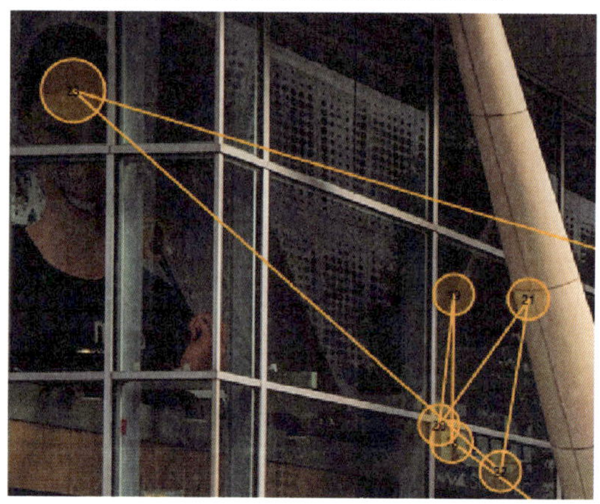

F The advertisement with a woman's face is latched onto immediately.

CONCLUSION

Recurrent scanpaths appear in the two streets in Manchester's Spinningfields. The eye seeks out places where it might expect to find people (see gazepath F). Written information, especially if relevant to the place, attract attention. Examples are posters on a door, the name of a business and street furniture with a map of the area.

Atkinson Street's modern frontage has adopted elements of the historical frontage opposite in an attempt to scale its mass to human proportions. The subdivided historical frontage (parcellization) is not active, but the positioning of the windows and doors and the wealth of detailing provide rhythm and attract many fixations. The balcony is an eye-catcher, effortlessly binding the two levels of the double-height frontage. Despite this, the participants rated Atkinson Street considerably lower than Hardman Street. The design solutions may help to mitigate the narrow street profile but do not seem able to compete with Hardman Street's wide profile, enhanced with fine paving, street furniture and greenery.

20
HY59 HJO

LONDON

MILLWALL

In recent decades London has made a concerted effort to densify and reach for the sky. The Isle of Dogs and Canary Wharf are just two well-known examples. Millwall is located on the Isle of Dogs. Interspersed between areas of high-rise are streets on a smaller, more intimate scale where the tall towers alternate with somewhat lower apartment buildings, as in the two streets selected for this study. But are they congenial spaces?

Millwall lies in a large meander of the River Thames, five kilometres east of the centre of London. The name refers to the windmills that stood on the river wall until the beginning of the nineteenth century when they made way for the factories of the industrial revolution and wharves were built along the riverbank. During the major economic transitions of the 1970s the factories closed down and in 1981 the London Docklands Development Corporation was set up to oversee the regeneration of the entire area.

STUDY AREA

Area size	16.2 ha	**Tallest building**	147 m
High-rise construction year	1981-2020*	**Height/width ratio Area average**	1:0.9
Population density	23.6k inh/km^2**		
Distance from centre	3 km	**Selected streets**	Millharbour Cassilis Road
Ground Space Index	0.4		

* *The twin-tower Pan Peninsula was completed in 2009 and in 2020 the Maine Tower welcomed its first residents.*

** *Population density of the entire Isle of Dogs*

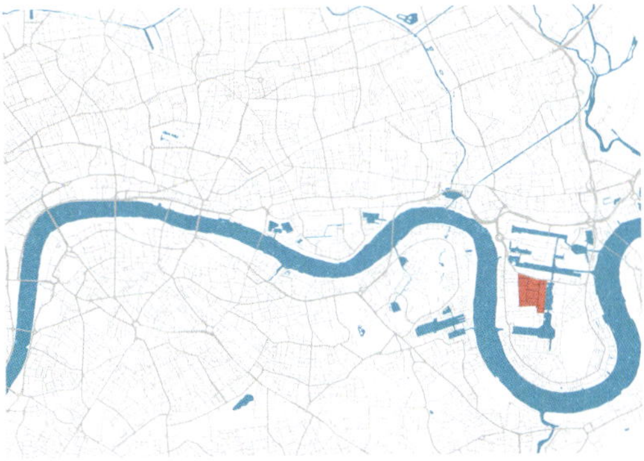

MORPHOLOGY

1 Millharbour
2 Cassilis Road

Buildings
Viewpoint

BUILDING HEIGHTS

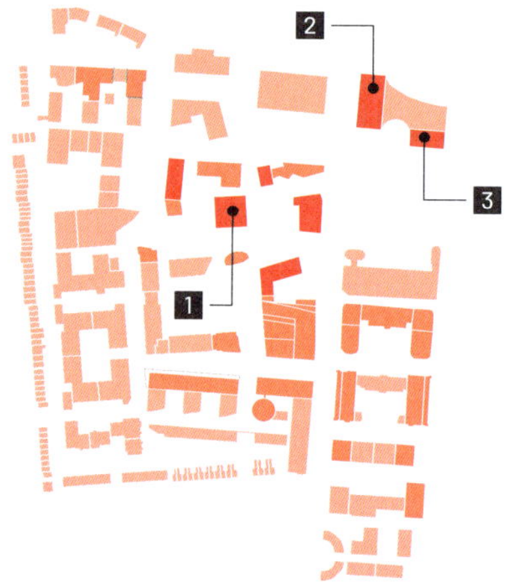

1 Maine Tower (144m)
2 Pan Peninsula (122m)
3 Pan Peninsula (147m)

Tall (80-150m)
Medium (30-80m)
Low (0-30m)

The area is partly redeveloped and partly still under development, as in Millharbour Village. The western redeveloped part of Millwall has a high concentration of (upmarket) apartment buildings and offices. In the north the area is bounded by Marsh Wall, which is also the boundary between Canary Wharf and Millwall, in the east by Inner Dock, on the south side by Mellish Street and on the west side by Alpha Grove. In terms of traffic Millwall is organized by a system of north-side access roads and secondary connecting east-west streets. The main points of connection with the city are on the north side where there are metro lines and the connection to roads leading to the centre of London.

The east side of the area, adjacent to Millwall Inner Dock, consists of a strip of large-scale housing complexes. Even the more loosely arranged complexes in the heart of the area are high-density and building heights rise towards the north in the direction of Canary Wharf. The small-scale row houses on the south and west side mark the shift in scale between the redeveloped and yet to be developed parts of Millwall. Many of the open outdoor areas belong to large-scale residential complexes and are hence semi-public in character.

MIXED-USE

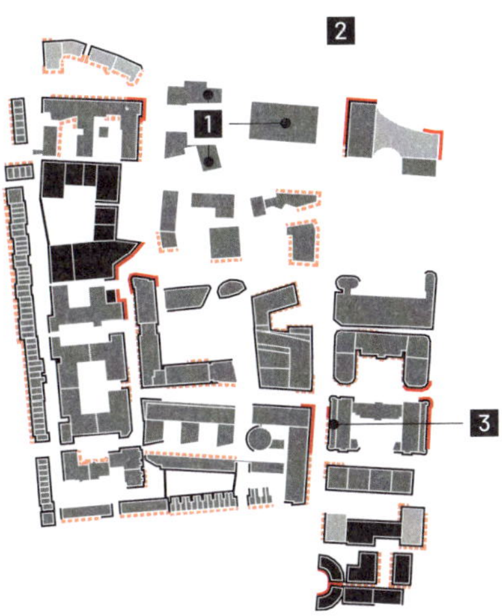

1 Millharbour Village
2 Canary Wharf
3 Tesco Supermarkt

Mix
Housing
Offices
Other
Closed GFL*
Active GFL*
Semi-active GFL*
Unknown

* Ground Floor Level

CONNECTIVITY

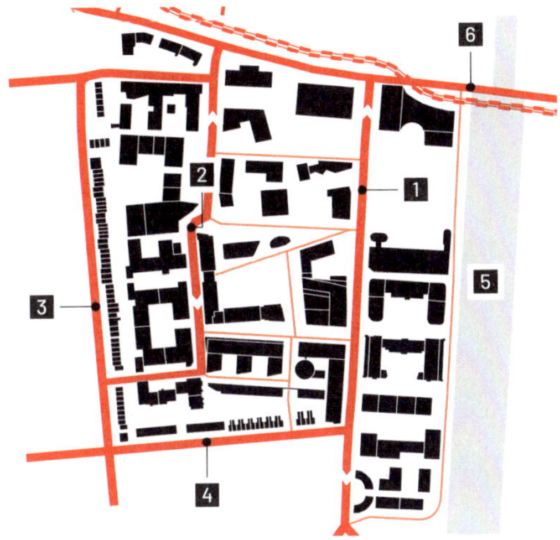

1 Millharbour
2 Cassilis Road
3 Alpha Grove
4 Mellish Street
5 Inner Dock
6 Marsch Wall

Main roads
Side roads
Railway/
Metro line

Building heights in the district rise steeply to the north and west. Currently two towers belonging to Pan Peninsula (122 and 147 metres/ 400 and 482 feet) are the tallest buildings on the peninsula, closely followed by the 2019 Main Tower (144 metres / 472 feet). Densification in the area is set to increase with the development of Millharbour Village in the north.

The functional mix consists of homes and offices, supplemented by commercial services at district level. The development of Millharbour Village will enrich that functional mix with 1500 new dwellings, 145,000 square metres of educational space, 63,000 square metres of commercial space plus several cultural facilities, including a theatre.

Along Millharbour, where a supermarket, coffee bar and a youth support organization sit side by side, the street fronts are active. People live and work here. In some places the street fronts are non-active. On Cassilis Road, which is primarily a residential street with dwellings at street level as well, they are mainly semi-active.

The two streets under examination here, Cassilis Road and Millharbour, are important access roads and begin at Marsh Wall. Although the streets have a similar apartment building programme, they are markedly different in character. Cassilis Road is more of a quiet residential street, whereas Millharbour is a busier street with a stronger mix of functions, higher density and taller buildings.

LiFE
20
Parcel Postbox
HY59 HJO

MILLHARBOUR

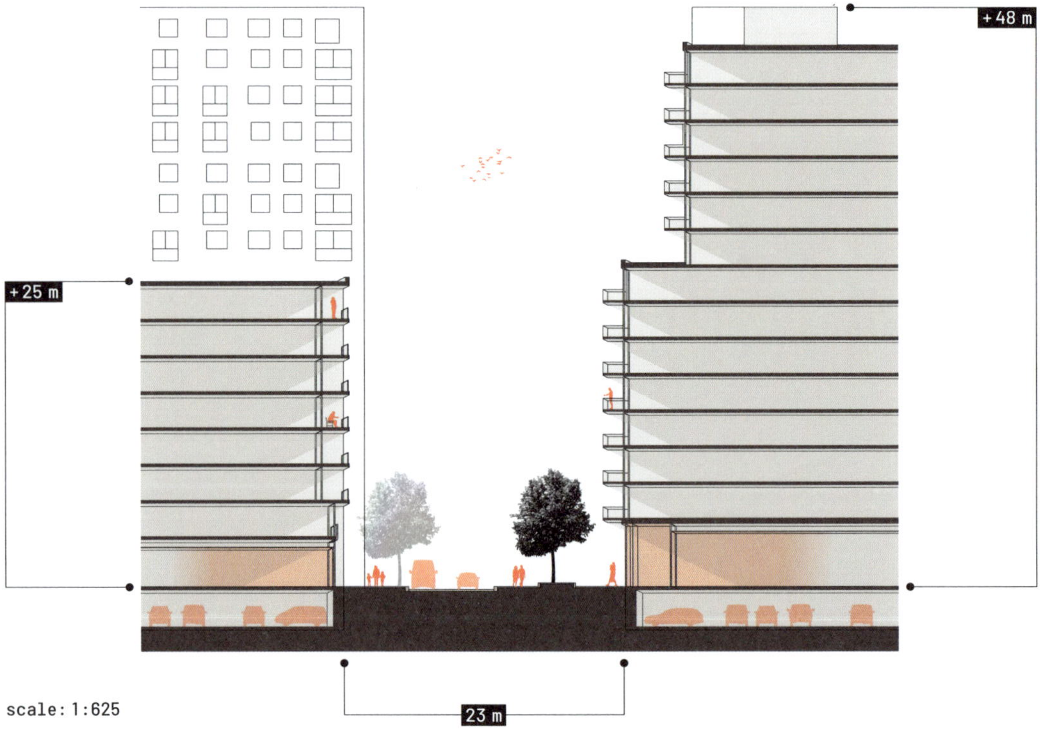

scale: 1:625

MILLHARBOUR

At the viewpoint the street profile broad relative to the height of the buildings and has a height-width ratio of 1:1.8. Moving northwards, the buildings on either side of Millharbour increase in height. From the viewpoint the street edges appear to be eight storeys high, but on the east side (right side in the images) the building is actually fifteen storeys: the top seven are set back. This setback benefits pedestrians whose importance is already acknowledged in the choice of parallel parking on one side only and a relatively narrow roadway. The street space is further enhanced with trees and paving.

Complex Streetscape

The Millharbour streetscape is visually complex, not only because of the way the buildings are positioned relative to one another, but also because of the wealth of architectural detailing. The width of the street profile ensures that the street gets plenty of light, air and space. Space that on the east side in particular contributes to pedestrian amenity via an arcade and a series of long tree planters.

Subtle Breaking up of Building Mass

Millharbour's street edges exhibit a wide variety of design solutions aimed at creating a human scale, beginning with the way the building masses are articulated, which is to say how the individual parts of the buildings are positioned relative to one another (see fig. Volume). In the foreground on the west side (left side in the images) the first two levels are set back in a concrete frame, giving rise to a two-storey frontage. An offset in the street edge also contributes to a subtle parcellation of the frontage.

The facades of the building beyond the narrow pedestrian lane are clad in a Tetris-like mosaic of different coloured cutouts. Together they create a pattern of zigzag lines designed to mitigate the scale of the building for pedestrians. This section, which is made up of small, glazed panels with a strong vertical orientation meets the street with a slightly set-back ground floor. On the east side the frontages are set back, and the overhang is supported by columns. Above street level a variety of setbacks are employed.

Soft Transition

The architectural variety is complemented by the diversity of ways in which the street space is cadenced. The facade on the west side, left in the foreground, is the most complex in terms of composition. It has a framework of concrete surrounds that generate space for a secondary articulation of French balconies in combination with alternating transparent and non-transparent facade sections. The building behind, with the flat facade, is more transparent in execution. Above the ground floor an apparently random distribution of narrow balconies commands attention.

On the east side (right side in the images) the elevation above street level is dominated by a horizontal articulation of wide balconies across the entire elevation. At street level it is the columns that provide verticality and rhythm.

DETAILS

1

3

2

4

The street front is transparent, with copious glass and entrances to a variety of commercial uses and to the entrance hall of the apartments above. Together it makes for a fine-grained appearance.

The frontages are clearly discernible along the entire street. They are overwhelmingly transparent and set back, like the building on the east side. This means that both street fronts are similar at eye level. There is, however, a big difference in pedestrian zones. The one on the east side is wider and is divided into two equal strips by the continuous tree planters. These also serve to soften the transition between building and street space, which is reinforced by the arcades. A similar effect is achieved on the west side by the frame-like recesses on the first two upper floors.

Hard Materials

Despite the space dedicated to pedestrians, the materials used in the street fronts - concrete, aluminium and sheet material - are relatively hard and predominantly flat. The buildings are undecorated, and the detailing is confined to the functional elements. A variety of outdoor spaces such as loggias and balconies provide the elevations with plasticity. In the design of the public space the different zones are distinguished by different types of relatively hard paving materials with a preponderance of grey tones.

BUILDING VOLUMES

GROUND FLOOR

STREET LEVEL

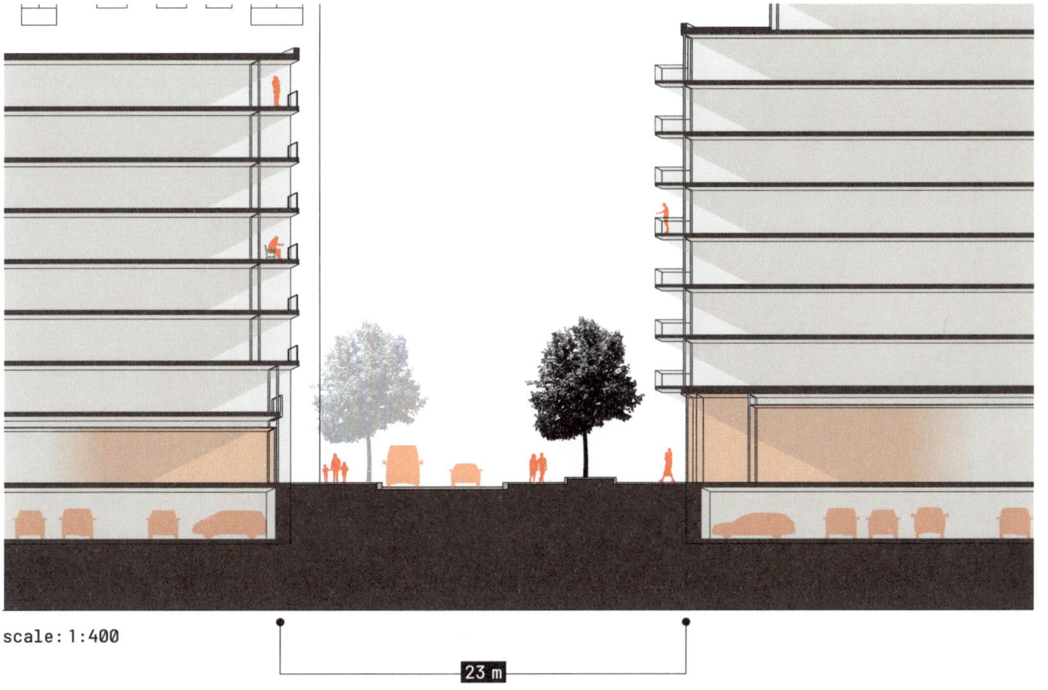

WD68 DPZ

CASSILIS ROAD

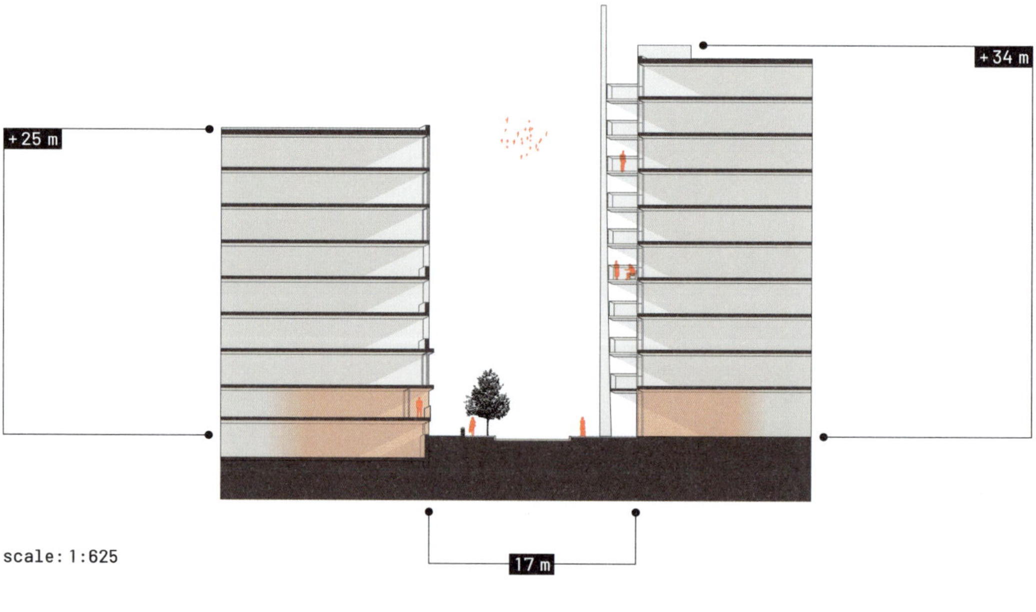

scale: 1:625

CASSILIS ROAD

The contrast between Cassilis Road and Millharbour in terms of profile (height-width ratio 1:1.6), scale and visual complexity is considerable. Cassilis Road, with its sober, restrained architecture and low-traffic streetscape, has a suburban feel. But a suburb where the street walls are eight storeys high and with housing at ground level. On the east side of the street the principle of the raised ground floor has been employed. On the west side the ground floor is set back, creating a covered pedestrian area in the form of an arcade.

Basic Structure

The buildings on either side of Cassilis Road are articulated according to a modern interpretation of conventional design solutions. On the west side (right side in the images) the gigantic piers of the building in foreground and the strips of brickwork flanked by balconies in the building beyond, provide a vertical articulation and a strong sense of depth.

By contrast, the east side (left side in the images) has a more horizontal articulation. The blocks of buildings are visually interrupted by a set-back section with continuous balconies and an underpass to a semi-private courtyard. The two-and-a-half storey base has a vertical window division that accentuates the individual dwellings. The facade architecture is fairly flat but at pedestrian level a modicum of plasticity is provided by the projecting frames and the set-back windows of the loggias.

Coherence

In terms of rhythm, the street is fairly traditional. As can be seen in the street profile, the raised ground floor of the bel étage on the east side of the street is the same height as the commercial ground floor on the west side. The pedestrian strip between the row of trees and the roadway is the same width as the strip between the piers and the roadway.

As in Millharbour, there is a design-driven coherence between street edge and public space. On the east side there is little direct physical contact between buildings and street space; on this side a transitional zone has been created by setting the buildings back from the building line. In the foreground this zone has been greened and bordered by a waist-high hedge of small shrubs. Rows of trees are often used to separate pedestrians from the traffic. Here shrubbery is used to give residents more privacy and to emphasize the small scale.

1

3

2

4

Closed Openness

The sand-coloured apartment block in the background of the images also features street-level housing. Most residents have screened their full-height windows with curtains or privacy film, turning a semi-active open ground floor into a closed one. The ground floor of the building on the west side is occupied by a local supermarket and a coffee bar. The transitional zones further along the street are ambiguous as it is not clear whether the space is private or public. Here, too, the residents have protected their privacy with curtains.

At eye level the street is dominated by the pedestrian space, which is physically separated from the residents' space by low hedges and green zones. The street wall on the east side is materialized in dark grey stucco interspersed with sheet material and light grey aluminium frames. Timber-like panels in the horizontal window bands provide a touch of warmth.

Boundaries

Further along the street the apartment block on the west side features sand-coloured brickwork in a smooth brick, in combination with light grey aluminium frames and galvanized steel railings. Frames have been used here, too. Executed in concrete they serve to distinguish the individual dwelling within the collective apartment building. The openwork corner of the apartment building on the west side at the end of this perspective marks the entrance to a side street access to which is regulated with a gate.

A hedge in combination with a row of trees provides a soft demarcation of public space on the east side. To reinforce the small scale of this area, the paving in the zone below the balconies is in a smaller tile and a different tile pattern compared with the paving on the west side between the piers and the roadway.

BUILDING VOLUMES

GROUND FLOOR

STREET LEVEL

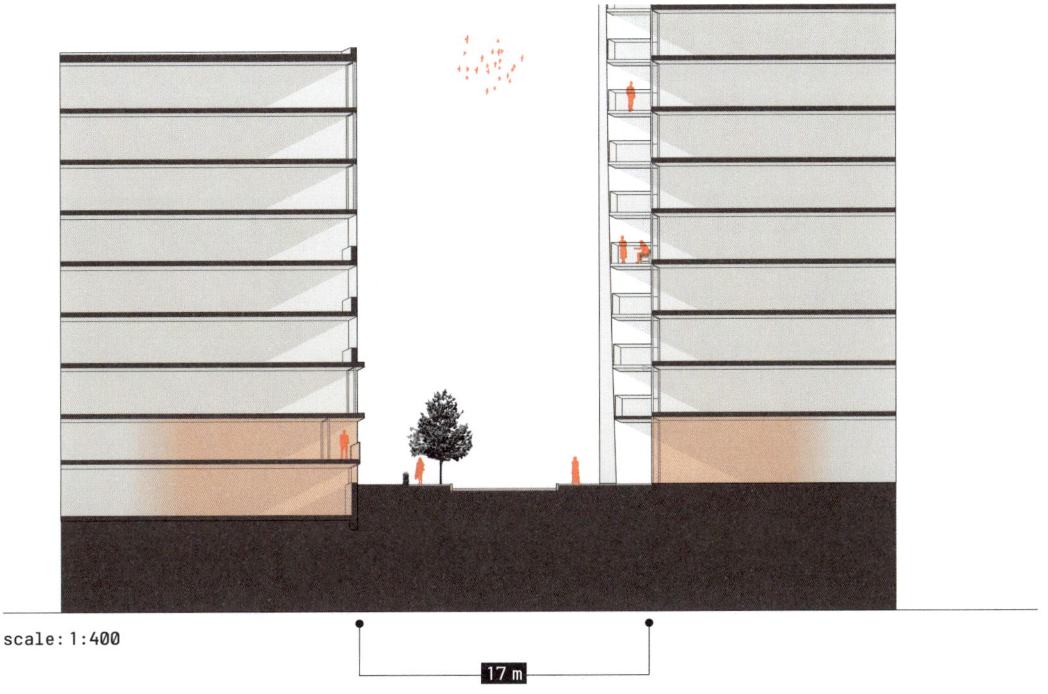

scale: 1:400

USER'S PERSPECTIVE

MILLHARBOUR

In both Millwall streets it is clear that in the design of buildings, street space and how buildings address the street space, detailed attention has been paid to the impact on users at eye level. This is evident in what attracts a viewer's attention. The participants in the neuroarchitecture test focused mainly on the active street ground floor, the trees and the business identification signs. Projecting elements attract more attention than more restrained recessed and set-back sections.

Millharbour illustrates this. The active street fronts on both sides of the street space are noticed by all, with the west side attracting particular attention. Here it is the balconies that attract a lot of eye fixations, whereas the balconies on the east side attract very little attention; the dark glass probably plays a role here.

One scanning pattern stands out: the building on the west side with the two-storey active ground floor in a concrete framework initially catches the eye, which is then led via the shallow French balconies to the many deep projecting balconies distributed across the building (see gazepath A). The balconies serve to visually connect the street walls at this height and in so doing enlarge the visual field (see gazepath B). At street level the eye is caught by the brightly coloured objects and also scans the cars and the tree (see gazepath C). Finally, the round forms of the building on the east side attract attention.

In Cassilis Road, compared with Millharbour, there is less interest in the ground floor. Attention quickly switches to the balconies of the buildings on the west side via the vertical strips

CASSILIS ROAD

of brickwork, with the eye moving back and forth (see gazepath D). The piers occasionally lead the eye to the third floor and higher (see gazepath E). The cars parked along the west side of the street and on the pavement on the east side attracted a lot of attention from the participants.

MILLHARBOUR

A The raised plinth draws the eye upwards.

B The dispersed balconies and high-rise result in a higher scanpath.

C Street furniture, bright colours, text and people is scanned in detail.

CASSILIS ROAD

D The eye scans across the balconies.

E The piers draw the line of sight upwards.

F Attention to separating greenery, shielding the houses behind it.

CONCLUSION

The numerous balconies and frames on both Millharbour and Cassilis Road in Millwall contribute visually to a relatable size and scale. The small green elements further increase the feeling of intimacy. The undemonstrative facade and screened ground floor openings on the west side of Cassilis Road were not noticed by many participants. The eye fixations were on greenery in front of the buildings that appears to work well as a soft separation between public and private space (see gazepath F). The eye was drawn to the more conspicuous apartment block on the other side of the street with its combination of tall piers, sand-coloured brickwork and balconies.

There is a subtle difference between the streets in terms of gazepaths and the speed of eye movements. The complexity of Millharbour evoked a more rapid, searching gaze than the calmer atmosphere of Cassilis Road. The test participants also rated Cassilis Road slightly higher than Millharbour.

OSLO

TJUVHOLMEN

Oslo is Norway's capital and, with 900,000 inhabitants, its biggest city. It is also a young city; in the nineteenth century fewer than 10,000 people lived there. The new district of Tjuvholmen is located on a two-part peninsula and is representative of Oslo's ambitious redevelopment of its waterfront. Each of the buildings, which were designed by over twenty different architectural practices, has its own distinct identity. The result is a concentrated representation of architectural solutions aimed at creating pleasant living environments in urban settings. In the Scandinavian climate the new district provides an intimate, sheltered street world.

Part of Oslo's nine-kilometre-long harbour promenade runs through Tjuvholmen. In summer the area is a popular place for land- and water-based recreation. The district consists of two small islands, Odden and Holmen, that are linked to the mainland by a central axis road. The name Tjuvholmen refers to 'Thieves' Island), the place where criminals were executed in the eighteenth century. In the early nineteenth century the island was enlarged with reclaimed land and used as a shipyard. Today the peninsula itself is free of cars but is accessible by car via a tunnel to which several parking garages are attached.

STUDY AREA

Area size	8.3 ha	**Tallest building**	84 m
High-rise construction year	2005-2014	**Height/width ratio** **Area average**	1:2.1
Population density	12.7k inh/km^2		
Distance from centre	0.5 km	**Selected streets**	Tjuvholmen Allé Sjøgangen
Ground Space Index	0.4		

MORPHOLOGY

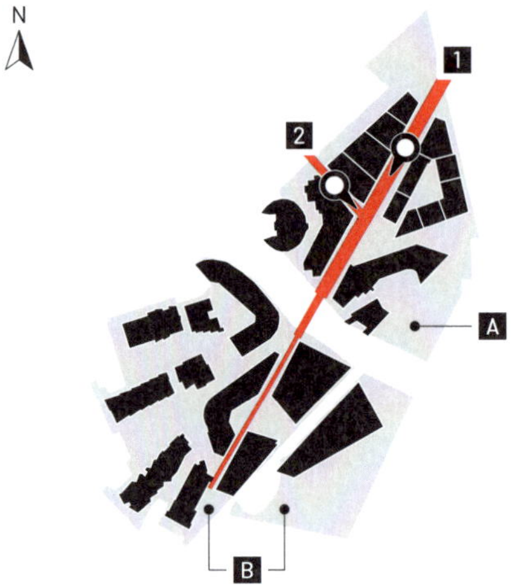

1 Tjuvholmen Allé
2 Sjøgangen
A Odden island
B Holmen island

Buildings
Island marking
Viewpoint

BUILDING HEIGHTS

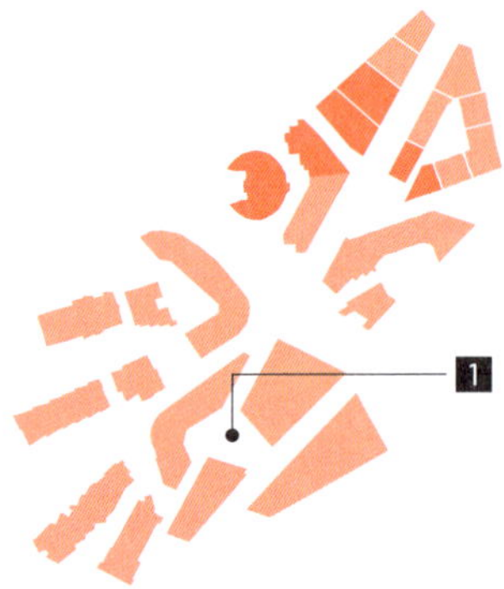

1 Viewing tower (90m)

Tall (80-150m)
Medium (30-80m)
Low (0-30m)

Since the 1980s Tjuvholmen has gradually developed into a more mixed area of housing, offices and commercial uses. In 2014 it became part of Fjord City, an ambitious urban renewal project aimed at redeveloping Oslo's waterfront. The project got underway in 2005 with the sale of land to developers.

The area has a good mix of uses, but there is little variation in the market segments served by those uses. Most of the dwellings and offices with underground parking are in the higher market segment and they are complemented by a luxury hotel called The Thief in reference to the original residents, and high-end restaurants, mostly located on the waterfront. Thanks to a waterside museum with lookout tower and sculpture garden, the neighbourhood is also a vibrant cultural and recreational destination that attracts visitors all year round.

The central Tjuvholmen Allé links both islands with the Aker Brygge neighbourhood. Running parallel to Tjuvholmen Allé, the narrow, more easterly Strandpromenaden provides an alternative link between Odden and Holmen. Both islands boast a central square. The buildings in Tjuvholmen are fairly similar in height, ranging from a minimum building height of eight storeys to twelve storeys. Density and building heights are greatest on both shores of the stretch of water separating Odden and Holmen.

Holmen is the second island and has several public functions. The street layout is fan-shaped with public spaces that open up to the waterfront. Running off Tjuvholmen Allé are side streets to the publicly accessible waterfront featuring a shoreline park, city beach and quaysides. On the southeast side lies the Strandhagen park and the

MIXED-USE

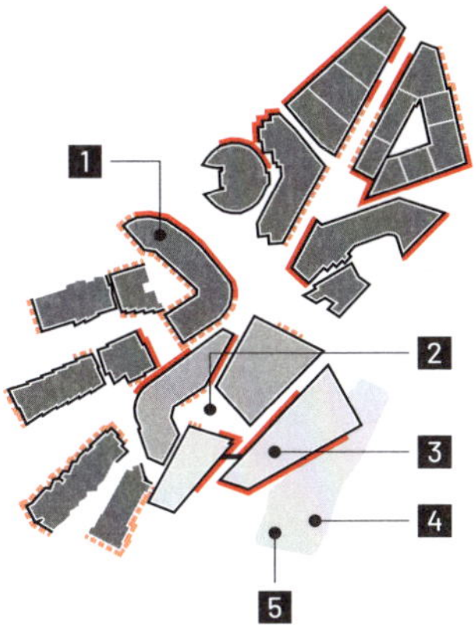

1 Hotel The Thief
2 Viewing tower
3 Astrup Fearnley Museum
4 Skulpturpark en Bystrand
5 Olav Selvaags Plass

Mix
Housing
Offices
Other
Closed GFL*
Active GFL*
Semi-active GFL*
Unknown

* Ground Floor Level

CONNECTIVITY

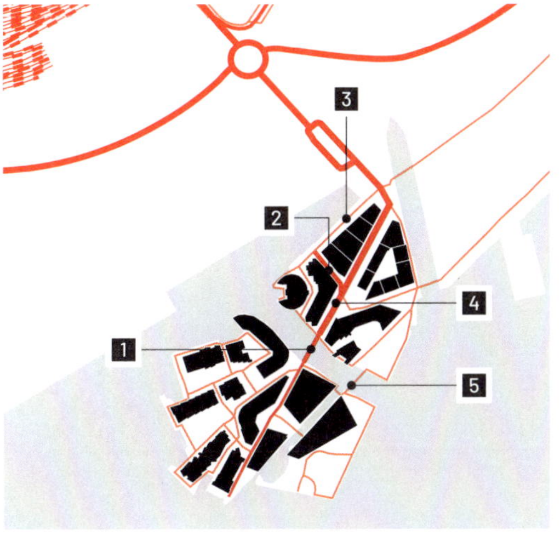

1 Tjuvholmen Allé
2 Sjøgangen
3 Bryggegangen
4 Tjuvholmen tunnel
5 Beach promenades

Main roads
Side roads
Railway/ Metro line

Astrup Fearly Museum of Modern Art designed by Renzo Piano, with the associated Tjuvholmen Sculpture Park. The south and southwest sides feature a paved boardwalk with public seating areas, and the municipal Tjuvholmen Sjobad.

Development on Tjuvholmen consists of clusters of larger buildings and building complexes. Odden Island consists almost entirely of housing and its street fronts are more active compared with Holmen. Anyone heading for Holmen passes through Odden on foot or by water because the peninsula is designed specifically for pedestrians and has numerous landing places for boats. On Odden, Tjuvholmen Allé is more commercial in character, while on Holmen there is a museum.

Tjuvholmen Allé is the backbone of both islands and one of the selected streets. There is evidence of 'wall formation', resulting in clearly defined public spaces. The elevations, which are divided into readily legible units, refer in scale to historical shopping streets. Sjøgangen, chosen as a kind of counterweight to Tjuvholmen Allé, is a narrow side street. On Odden it links the canalside Bryggegangen street with Olav Selvaags square. While Tjuvholmen Allé is the link with the mainland, Sjøgangen connects the waterside with the urban centre and vice versa.

TJUVHOLMEN ALLÉ

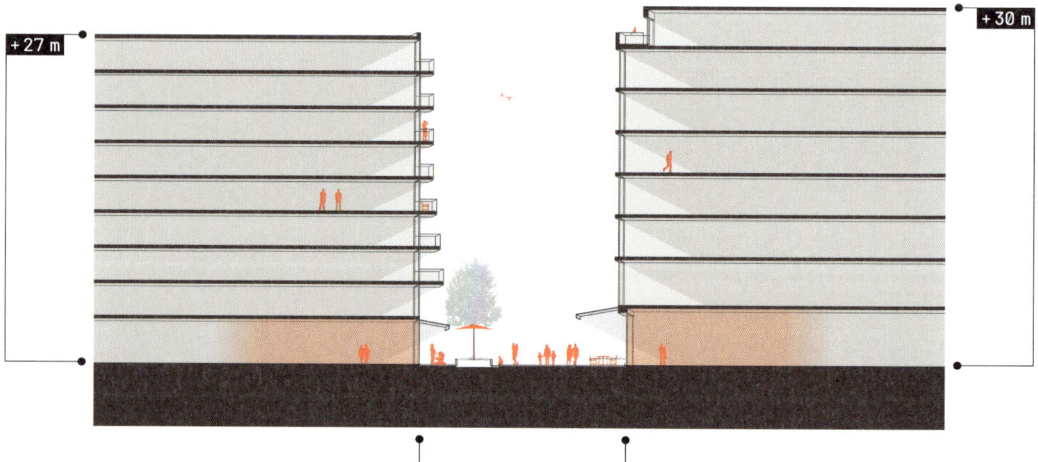

scale: 1:625

TJUVHOLMEN ALLÉ

Tjuvholmen Allé is the backbone of the area. Our focus is on the section of the street on the island of Odden, where development consists mostly of housing. The street has a height-width ratio of 1:1.8, with street walls from eight to nine storeys high. The street walls enclose the street space, which is designed with the pedestrian in mind. It is divided into three parts: public and commercial open spaces along the edges, traffic in the middle. The result is a wide pedestrian zone that can cope with large visitor flows and that provides access to the various zones.

Visual Parcellation of the Street Edges

The street edges appear to be made of individual 'buildings' resulting in a streetscape with a fair amount of architectural diversity. The street fronts are two storeys high, and the ground floor has been activated with shops and restaurants. The street edges are clad with a lot of glass and sheet material as well as metal and concrete. All these materials have a flat, smooth surface but the facades nevertheless display a high degree of plasticity thanks to the detailing; examples include the balconies, protruding horizontal bands, vertical and horizontal strips and overhangs.

The visual parcellation of the street edges breaks their mass up into individual units, but the units on the northwest side (left side in the images) are clearly larger than those on the southeast side (right side in the images), which consequently seem to be smaller. The balconies on the northwest side catch the eye thanks to their partially 'undulating' design, while on the other side the facades tend to be flatter. The street front on the southeast side is interrupted by an archway leading to a semi-private courtyard with underground car park.

Active Ground Floor

The rhythm in the street is strongly defined by the mostly vertical articulation of the street front. The facade sections above have a primary horizontal articulation plus a secondary vertical articulation in the form of vertical slats. The horizontal lines are sustained in the street space with a series of rectangular tree planters. Most of the often two-storey street fronts are transparent. Because each 'unit' has at least one publicly accessible entrance, the street wall has a high degree of permeability, a strong rhythm and variation. However, the street edge and street space merge without any mediating elements.

DETAILS

1

3

2

4

Small-scale Effect

Owing to the focus on pedestrians, a lot of attention has been paid to designing a street space that conjures a small-scale feeling so as to counterbalance the combination of relatively large building volumes and a narrow street. The transition from street edge to street space has been handled by dividing the public space into three: a continuous (pedestrian) traffic zone in the centre, flanked by two transitional zones intended for places to linger. On the southeast side these take the form of geometric tree planters edged with seating; on the northwest side they translate into outdoor dining areas. Thus the street provides both open public and semi-public (commercial) spaces for people to congregate and linger. The street fronts respond directly with a high degree of transparency, contrasting facade compositions and retractable awnings.

The materialization is diverse and multi-layered. The elevations are characterized by a high degree of transparency in combination with a variety of sheet materials. Metal and concrete are also used. A relatively rich facade detailing helps to enliven the predominantly flat and smooth materials. For example, the red colour of the panels on the building on the northwest side ensures that the facade stands out, while a pattern of round holes breaks up the monotonous surface. That was probably the intention, whether it is actually perceived as such only the neuroarchitecture test can tell us.

BUILDING VOLUMES

GROUND FLOOR

STREET LEVEL

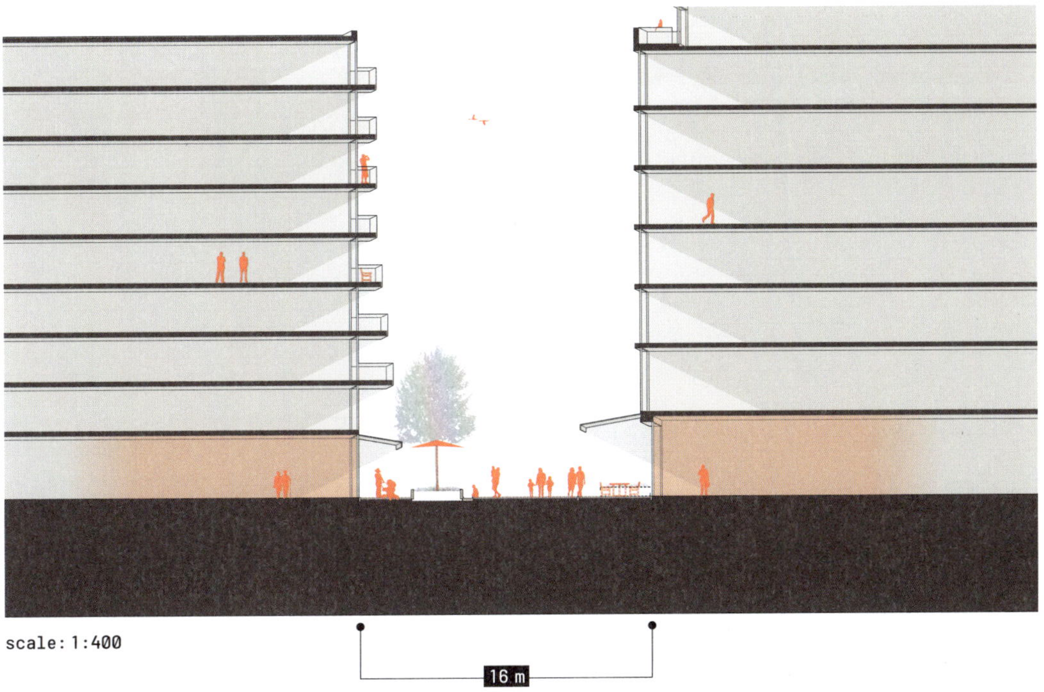

Pedestrians are Key

Diversity is also evident in the public space. Different types of paving in different patterns and aligned with the different zones have been employed to provide additional detailing. The central open space is paved in large tiles alternated with strips of narrower clinker bricks, which makes Tjuvholmen Allé seem wider than it is. The transitional zones along both street edges are clearly articulated with clinkers laid in a running bond. On the southeast side the designers opted for small round planters, while on the northwest side the transitional zone is defined by large tree planters and a gutter.

This concealed gutter serves not only as a drain and boundary but also as a continuous line in the paving, subtly connecting the various parts of the street. Stylish street lighting, rubbish bins and bollards are in the same dark grey colour as the other street furniture. The tree planters are a combination of concrete and wood for the benches. They contain small trees and a single species of ground cover. Concrete planters have been integrated into the northwest zone.

SJØGANGEN

scale: 1:625

SJØGANGEN

While Tjuvholmen Allé is the most important thoroughfare on both islands, the much narrower Sjøgangen is typical of the maze of streets connecting the active outer edges of the islands with the urban centres. Sjøgangen runs between the quayside promenade of Bryggegangen and Olav Selvaags Square. The viewpoint is towards Tjuvholmen Allé. Like most of the cross streets in Tjuvholmen, Sjøgangen is narrow and its 1:4.5 height-width ratio leaves little scope for pedestrian zone embellishment. What is more, the buildings appear closed, so what has been done to turn it into a pleasant walkway?

Main Structure

The street profile reveals a difference in scale between the two street walls. The southern wall (right side in the images) is a huge, thirteen-storey hotel building, while the office building opposite rises to nine storeys. Both sides have shallow overhangs above street level. The narrow street profile intensifies the feeling of enclosure for pedestrians. From this viewpoint the street terminates at Olav Selvaags Square where two-storey, projecting frames form the transition from street to square. Dividing the street frontage up in this way draws attention to important functions like entrances and windows.

On the south side the eye is immediately drawn to the sharply indented street wall, which is executed in white stucco and has recessed window frames. The ground floor is set forward here which serves to break the long street edge into smaller, recognizable modules from the viewpoint of the pedestrian. Relief is introduced to the whole with the subtle offsetting of the street-level windows and deep reveals. The resulting vertical articulation provides pedestrians with a sense of rhythm.

Secondary Street

The street front on the north side (left side in the images) is quite different. Here horizontal concrete bands create a very horizontal and flat impression. Although the street front appears to be transparent, it cannot really be termed active. The various doors are secondary entrances for deliveries and emergency exits. Most of the windows have been obscured and an inner wall has been placed directly behind the windows. This is true of the entire street. On the hotel side, areas in front of windows are used for bicycle parking or windows have been obscured.

The materials used here are predominantly flat, smooth and cold. The office building facade consists of grey, concrete-like cladding and pale grey aluminium frames. The ground floor frontage includes a double door, but it has not been articulated to signal 'entrance' to passers-by because the main entrance is on the city square side of Sjøgangen.

DETAILS

1

3

2

4

Subtle Solutions

On both sides there has been an attempt to make a connection between the street front and the street space. On the north side via transparency in the form of an aluminium lower front. On the south side with a zigzagging frontage that generates a modicum of engagement between street space and frontage.

A great deal of detailing has been used on the ground floor of the hotel. The standing vertical seams of the aluminium cladding and the slightly projecting dark stone frontage provide a high degree of tactility. The soffits of the triangular overhangs are in the same white stucco as the facade and have integrated light fittings. Although this is a narrow street, such design interventions prevent it from being dark and obscure. The lines in the paving provide a subtle sense of direction to pedestrians.

BUILDING VOLUMES

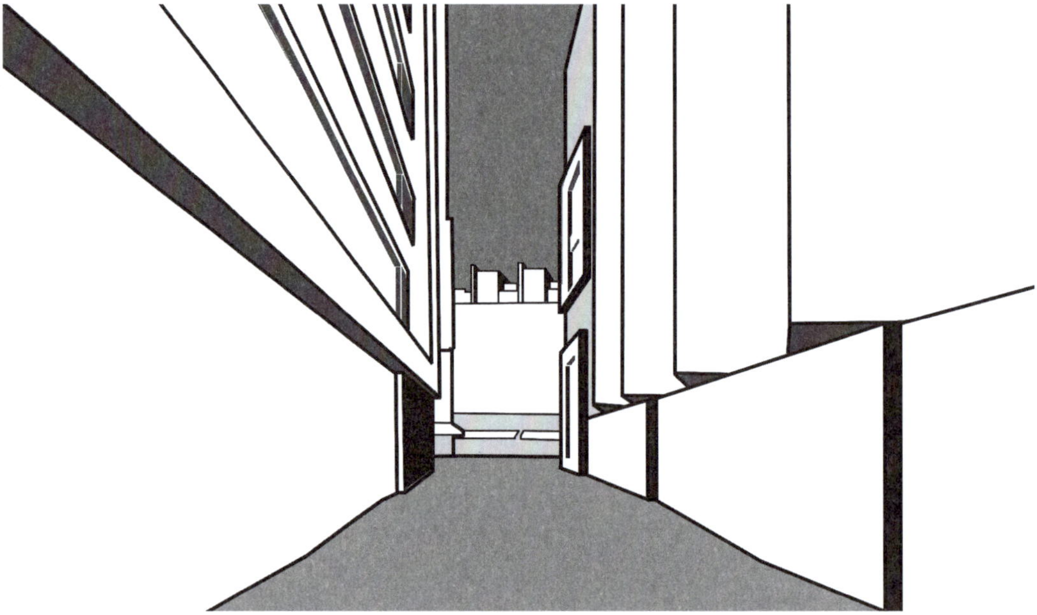

GROUND FLOOR

STREET LEVEL

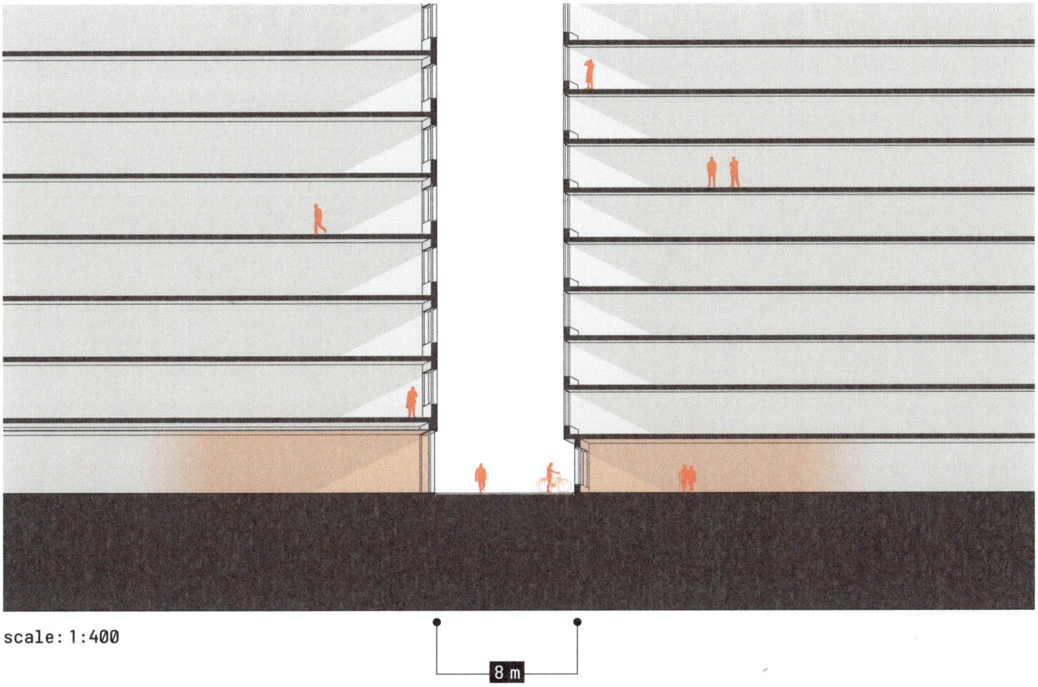

scale: 1:400

USER'S PERSPECTIVE

TJUVHOLMEN ALLÉ

Whereas Tjuvholmen Allé is the backbone of the two islands, Sjøgangen is typical of the many laneways that connect the islands' inner area with the waterside and adjacent restaurants. These differences were reflected in the visual experience of the participants in the neuroarchitecture test.

In Tjuvholmen Allé the design solutions aimed at scaling the street space have had the desired effect. The fine grain of the transitional spaces between the building and the street is certainly reflected in viewing behaviour (see heatmaps). People scanned the street fronts and on the northwest side this usually took in the tree planters that mark the transitional boundary (see gazepath A). The steps, greenery and signage are favourite fixation points. On the southeast side the greened entrance stands out. From there the gaze follows the more or less continuous horizontal articulation of these buildings in a fairly linear trajectory (see gazepath B). At the same time the buildings on the horizon attract attention. They stand on a square-like space where the buildings appear from behind a setback building line (see gazepath C).

In Sjøgangen by contrast the viewing behaviour is more tentative. The eyes glide past the walls and scan places where people might be, such as the dark windows of the hotel, the framed doors at ground level and the windows overlooking the street. Because of the positioning of the windows in the zigzag facade the gaze is inevitably drawn upwards above street level (see gazepath D and E). On the other hand, the slight overhang of this hotel building redirects the eye downwards to street level (see gazepath E).

SJØGANGEN

In Sjøgangen, as in Tjuvholmen Allé, there is one building in the distance that attracts attention (see gazepath F). The street is short so this building at the end, perpendicular to the street, is clearly visible. The ground floor and the balconies in particular catch and hold the attention. The termination of the visual field, with a building at right angles results in a compact, circular eye-movement pattern. There is less interest in the street itself, which is fairly bare and simply laid out.

Also noteworthy are the places and elements that receive less attention. On Tjuvholmen Allé, for example, the ninety-metre Tjuvitten viewing tower is visible in the distance, but it fails to catch the eye.

TJUVHOLMEN ALLÉ

A The eye is guided by the active front and the rhythmical line of tree planters.

B The horizontal articulation guides the eye and thus also the pedestrian.

C The eye is drawn to the contours of buildings in the distance.

SJØGANGEN

D The slight overhang results in brief fixations on the street front.

E The staggered ground floor and indented facade generate a wealth of fixations.

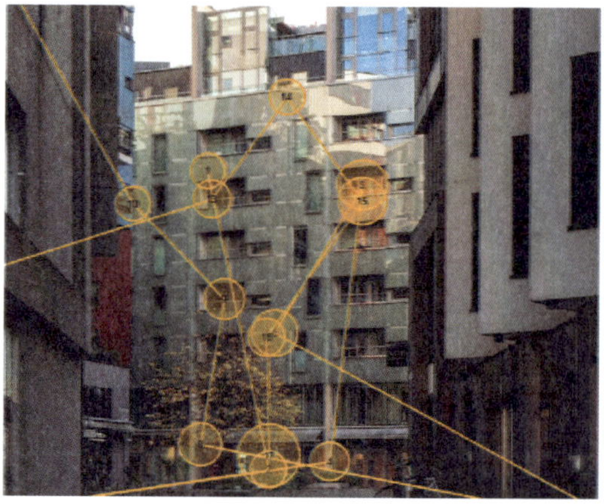

F The wide openings of the building in the distance attract attention.

CONCLUSION

Tjuvholmen has been laid out with pedestrians in mind, with continuous street fronts and a clearly defined public space and that is evident in the two streets in the study, Tjuvholmen Allé and Sjøgangen. Combinations of design solutions aimed at pedestrians attracted the attention of the participants. The scanpath is neither searching nor hasty; the gaze is guided and expands at eye level.

There are also differences linked to the fact that Tjuvholmen Allé, despite a massive street wall and narrow street space, has a clear social function. Visual attention focuses on the small-scale elements in the street space. The subtly layered transitions between facade and street appear to work well here. Unsurprisingly, of all the streets in the study Tjuvholmen Allé was the most highly rated.

Sjøgangen was given an average rating, which is impressive given that its sole function is as a link between a public square and popular waterside. If there were no large open spaces on either side of this short street it would have a claustrophobic quality. But the combination of design solutions in the street itself – frames, overhanging white-stuccoed triangles with dark window frames – breaks up the entire street wall and introduces rhythm, and this is reflected in the scanpaths. It remains a pleasant laneway to walk down.

AMSTERDAM

ZUIDAS

Amsterdam Zuidas is an urban hub with world-class high-rise buildings. It is strategically located close to Schiphol Airport and walking distance from the old well-to-do districts of Amsterdam. Since this prestigious area development project began in 1998, ambitions have gradually shifted from a primarily international business location for financial and business services and corporate headquarters to a metropolitan live-work location. That shift is reflected in the two selected streets: the area's central access road flanked by office and apartment buildings (Gustav Mahlerlaan) and a genuine residential street (George Gershwinlaan).

As the capital of the Netherlands Amsterdam has a long tradition of large-scale spatial developments. The Zuidas development got under way in 1998 with the headquarters of the ABN AMRO Bank. The underlying concept was influenced by financial districts like Canary Wharf in London, which borders the previously discussed Millwall. Meanwhile further development is aimed at a mixed metropolitan area.

STUDY AREA

Area size	15.7 ha	**Tallest building**	105 m
High-rise construction year	1998-2020*	**Height/width ratio Area average**	1:1.8
Population density	12.1k inh/km^2		
Distance from centre	0.8 km	**Selected streets**	Gustav Mahlerlaan George Gershwinlaan
Ground Space Index	0.4		

* *In 1998, following the ABN AMRO bank's decision to build its head office here, the city developed a spatial masterplan for the area. The George (2020) put the finishing touch to George Gershwinlaan.*

MORPHOLOGY

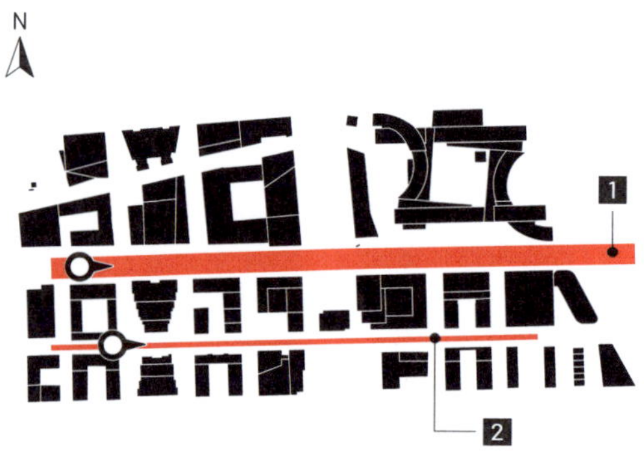

1 Gustav Mahlerlaan
2 George Gershwinlaan

Buildings
Viewpoint

BUILDING HEIGHTS

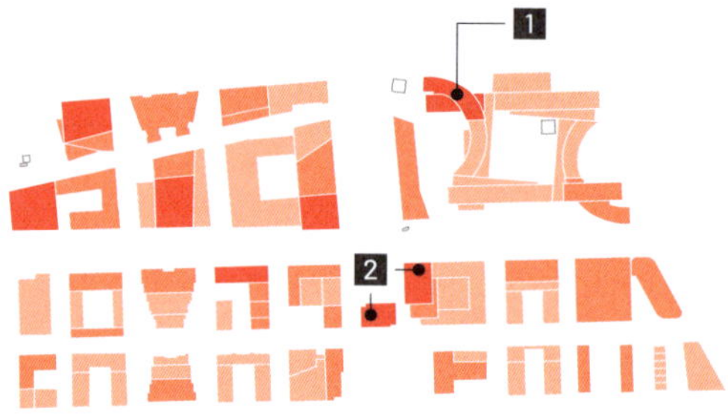

1 ABN AMRO head office (105m)
2 Amsterdam Symphony (97-105m)

Tall (80-150m)
Medium (30-80m)
Low (0-30m)

The Zuidas is a decades-long project, and the masterplan has been revised and updated several times. The current 2016 version (Gemeente Amsterdam 2016) covers continued development up to 2030, adding some 3.4 million square metres (currently 2 million m^2).

Although the Zuidas is still substantially a financial-legal business district, it is becoming more diverse with the arrival of other businesses such as tech companies. Several office buildings are under construction and Tripolis-Park, the 'horizontal skyscraper' housing Uber's international headquarters, was recently completed. Right now office space accounts for three times as much volume as housing, but this is set to change dramatically in the coming years with the construction of many more new dwellings. Ravel, a new car-free residential area with 1,350 dwellings, is currently being built. Also new is the forty per cent social housing goal and the focus on families. This makes it all the more important to realize an attractive, human living environment in amongst that high density/high-rise setting; to create a place that is equally good to be in outside office hours. That ambition is clearly reflected in the design choices.

This analysis focuses on the section of Zuidas south of the A10 ring road. The morphological map reveals that the area is actually made up of four quadrants, underpinned by the main thoroughfare Gustav Mahlerlaan in the east-west direction and perpendicular to a pedestrian route encompassing three public squares that runs from the Amsterdam Zuid station in the north to De Boelegracht in the south. The building blocks north of Gustav Mahlerlaan have a larger urban grain than those on the south side. The northeast quadrant is defined by the (former) ABN AMRO Bank complex and the round CIRCL pavilion on Gustav Mahler Square. The northwest quadrant is characterized by large-scale office buildings, intersected by a diagonal pedestrian route. The two southern quadrants consist primarily of compact apartment blocks.

MIXED-USE

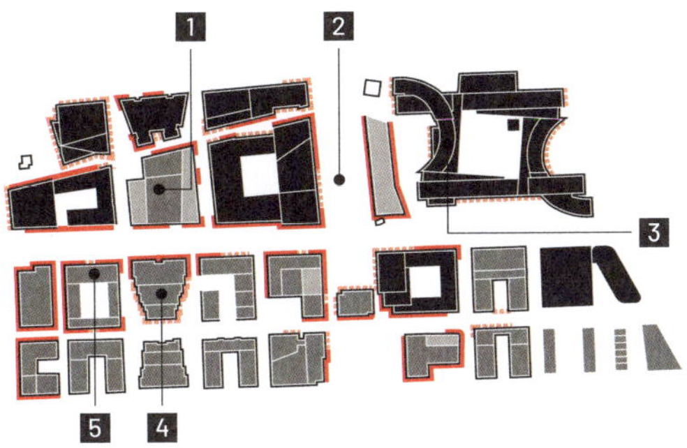

1 New Amsterdam
2 Gustav Mahlerplein
3 ABN AMRO bank
4 Summertime
5 900 Mahler

- Mix
- Housing
- Offices
- Other
- Closed GFL*
- Active GFL*
- Semi-active GFL*
- Unknown

* Ground Floor Level

CONNECTIVITY

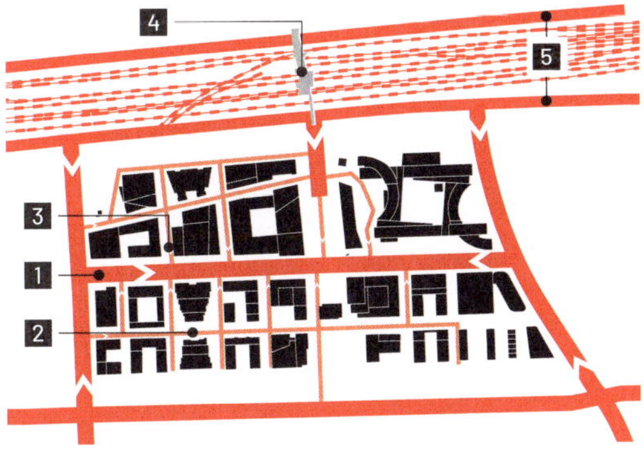

1 Gustav Mahlerlaan
2 George Gershwinlaan
3 Benjamin Brittenstraat
4 Amsterdam Zuid Station
5 A10 Motorway

- Main roads
- Side roads
- Railway/ Metro line

The Zuidas grid structure is made up of a system of primary east-west main throughfares and north-south connecting streets. The latter are used to accommodate ancillary functions like the entrances to underground car parks, logistics and mechanical services. As well as being the main east-west connection in the Zuidas, Gustav Mahlerlaan links into the city's road network.

A focal point of the area is the intersection between Gustav Mahlerlaan and the north-south pedestrian zone, which includes a succession of three public squares. The centrally located train, bus and metro station Amsterdam Zuid functions as a public transport hub and important entrance point for the Zuidas.

The elevation map of the grid reveals a checker-board distribution of tall and low buildings. The Zuidas has very few standalone towers; high-rise accents are usually part of a larger block – in line with the new hybrid urban block typology. Land-marks in the southern part of the Zuidas include Amsterdam Symphony I (105 metres / 344 feet), Amsterdam Symphony II (97 metres / 318 feet) and the (former) ABN AMRO head office (105 metres / 344 feet).

The area boasts a rich mix of uses that includes a variety of commercial and non-commercial facilities in addition to offices and housing. On the north side of Gustav Mahlerlaan offices with ground-floor commercial uses predominate, on the south side apartment buildings with for the most part semi-active ground floors.

This analysis focuses on two parallel streets with different characters and functions. Gustav Mahlerlaan is the main access road for motorized traffic while George Gershwinlaan is residential and geared to pedestrian traffic.

ZG-376-V
Htel

GUSTAV MAHLERLAAN

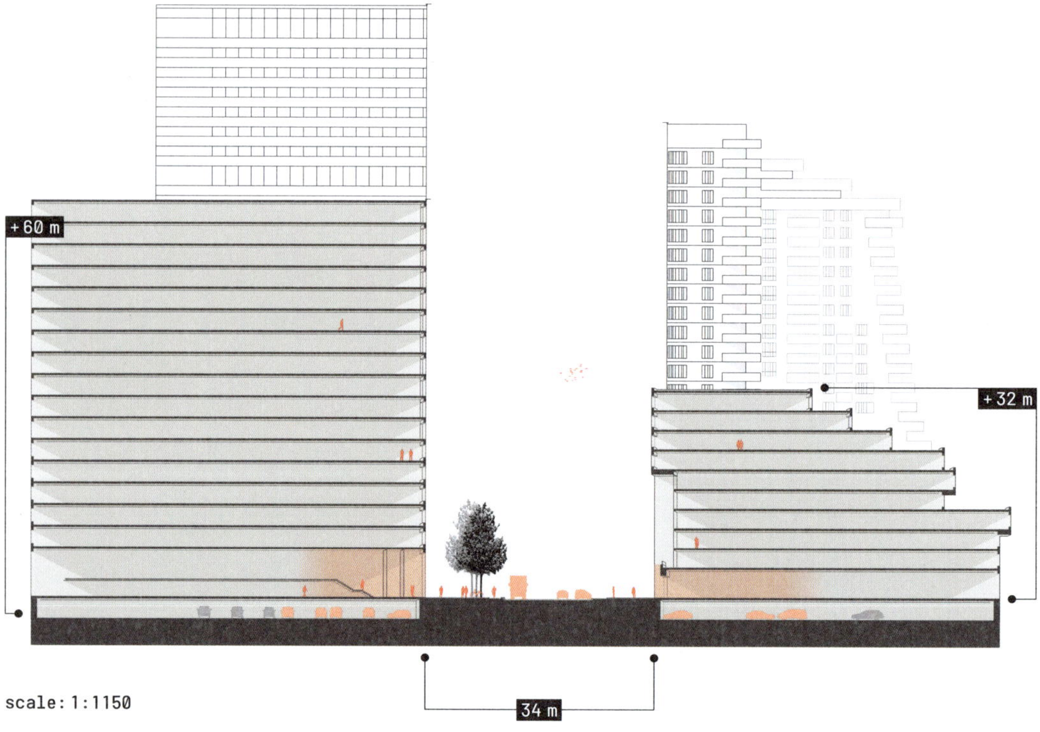

scale: 1:1150

GUSTAV MAHLERLAAN

The Zuidas grid concept of tall and low buildings is also evident in the street profile of Gustav Mahlerlaan. Like Millharbour in London and Tjuvholmen Allé in Oslo, it has a height-width ratio of 1:1.8. The two street walls differ greatly in height. Despite the street's important traffic function, there is also consideration for pedestrians and slower traffic. The buildings are bordered by relatively wide pedestrian zones flanked by a row of trees and further screened from the motorized traffic by cycle lanes that are not part of the roadway.

Big Contrasts

Diversity is expressed in the Gustav Mahlerlaan streetscape in the building forms and heights. There is a notable difference in architecture between the north and south side of the street. The north side (left in the images) is lined by functional architecture, mostly offices, whereas the south side (right side in the images) consists mainly of brick-built apartment buildings.

The variation in building heights is clearly visible and the buildings that together make up the streetscape exhibit a high degree of diversity, including in their basic structure. There is a mix of podium-towers, stepped building masses and traditional, taut building volumes. A row of medium-sized trees brings unity and rhythm to the north side of the street space and filters the street-level view of the larger building volumes.

Solutions at the Level of the Building

While facade articulation on the north side is predominantly horizontal, the south side displays greater architectural diversity. 900 Mahler takes its inspiration from early twentieth-century apartment buildings in Manhattan. It contains high-end apartments and is set apart by a strong vertical articulation all the way down to the street; the top of the three-storey podium is also articulated. The brickwork is used to break up the mass of the podium and to create a three-dimensional play of vertical and (recessed) horizontal lines.

The neighbouring sculptural Summertime apartment block consists chiefly of mid-priced rental apartments. Its main entrance is marked by a tall vertical incision in the building mass. In common with most of the other buildings on this side its base has not been distinguished in any way, apart from the six-storey 'bite' taken out of the facade for the main entrance. The facade above the recessed entrance consists of a glass curtain wall and coloured tiles. This succeeds in breaking up the mass of the building, but it is questionable whether this delivers a sense of intimacy. The building's sides have cantilevered loggias. Because the horizontally articulated facades on the north side of Gustav Mahlerlaan display little plasticity, these balconies are particularly noticeable and so also the side street (Benjamin Brittenstraat) they overlook.

DETAILS

Accentuated Entrances

The bases of the buildings on both sides of Gustav Mahlerlaan are two to three storeys high and are differentiated from the floors above by a greater degree of transparency. The entrances to buildings have been accentuated in the street frontage in a number of ways. For example, the main entrance of the New Amsterdam podium-tower on the north side is marked by a combination of columns and a two storey setback.

Both New Amsterdam and Summertime have a multi-level central lobby that seeks to engage with the street space and effectively acts as a continuation of the public space. In other buildings awnings are used to mark the main entrance. In addition to commercial uses, the multi-storey podiums on the south side of Gustav Mahlerlaan contain the main entrances to the apartment buildings.

Most of the buildings on the south side of Gustav Mahlerlaan are executed in dark brick, whereas glass and whitish cladding panels predominate on the north side. This is a reflection of the programmatic differences between the two sides: office buildings to the north versus apartment buildings to the south. The wide footpaths and cycle paths are paved with the same type of tile but in different colours so as to distinguish between the almost level zones for slow traffic.

BUILDING VOLUMES

GROUND FLOOR

STREET LEVEL

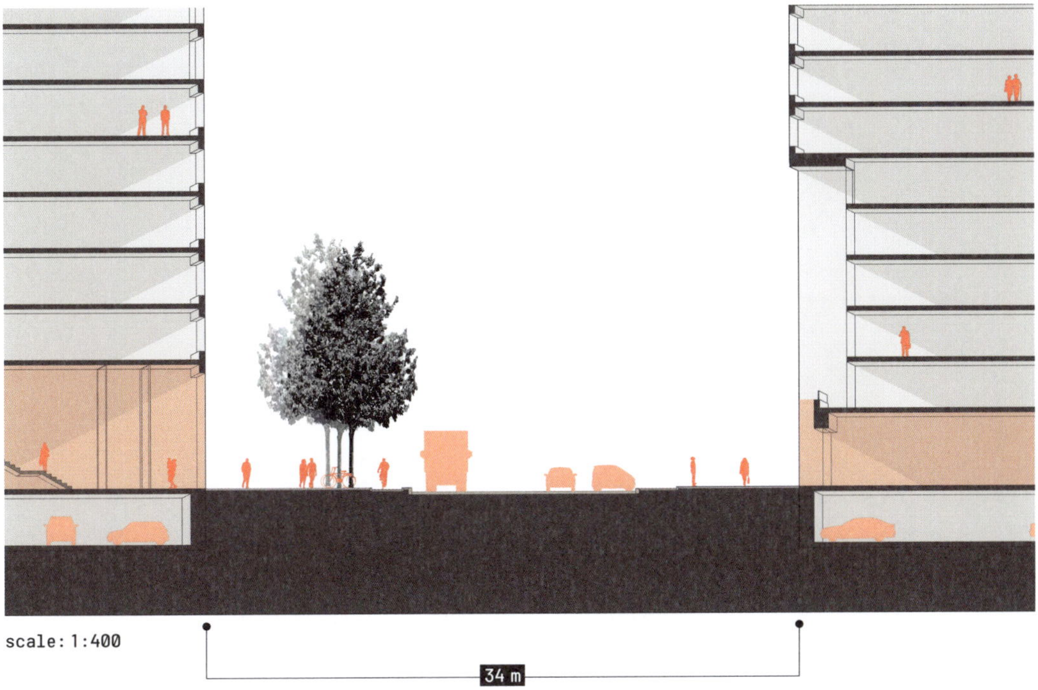

GEORGE GERSHWINLAAN

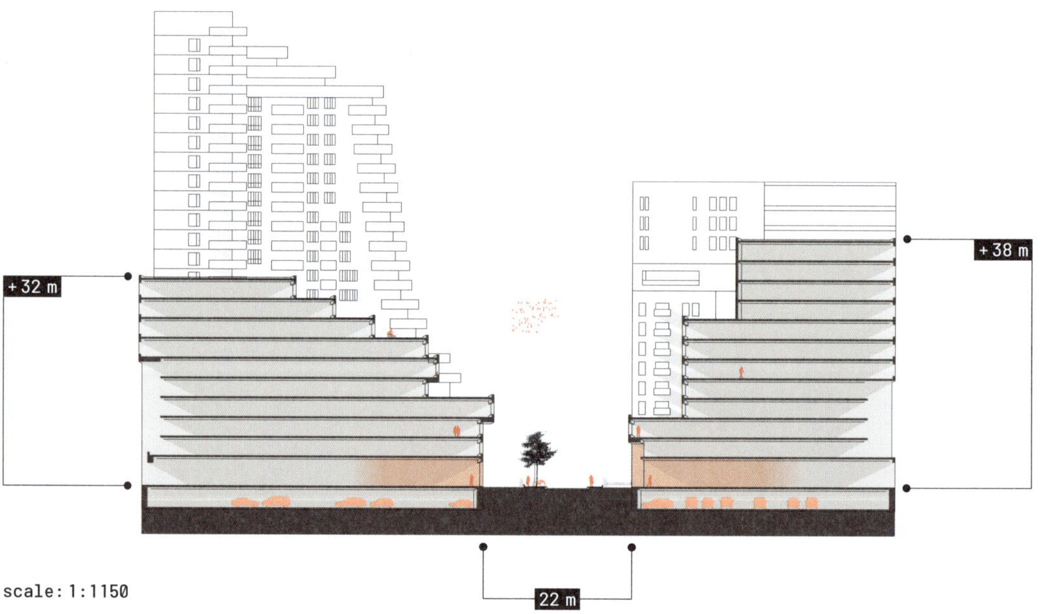

scale: 1:1150

GEORGE GERSHWINLAAN

Unlike Gustav Mahlerlaan, George Gershwinlaan is a dedicated residential street. Not only are the buildings here more fine-grained than the offices on Gustav Mahlerlaan, but they are also considerably lower. This delivers a height-width ratio of 1:1.6, comparable to that of Cassilis Road. It is clear that pedestrians have priority here: the roadway is designed for local traffic only. The streetscape is characterized by an absence of on-street parking, the use of greenery along property edges and the presence of a pocket park.

Light, Air and Space

The building mass along George Gershwinlaan is defined by the prevalence of setbacks. This makes it seem as though the street space is bordered by three to four storey buildings, resulting in plenty of light, air and space. Whether the participants in the neuroarchitecture test see it this way remains to be seen. The street walls are not continuous, but there is a lot of variation in building heights and building typology, which results in an open and permeable streetscape.

Facade depth has been achieved in a variety of ways. Often through interlocking and cantilevering volumes topped by balconies. Three-dimensionality is introduced by incisions in the building mass for a main entrance and coloured balcony screens. In a nod to the financial world, the colour scheme for these screens refers to old Dutch banknotes. The lilac-coloured screens on Gustav Mahlerlaan refer to the lighthouse on the 250 guilder note while the greenish-yellow of the screens on George Gershwinlaan was inspired by the sunflower on the 50 guilder note.

Mountain-like Building Volumes

Some buildings feature a 'classic' articulation, such as the 105-metre (344 foot) Amsterdam Symphony I tower that acts as an orientation point in the street. The building on the south side, in the foreground of the pictures, uses traditional techniques such as a transparent, vertically articulated base terminated by a horizontal band. Summertime's sculptural, alp-like volumes make use of another technique. Here the street wall is articulated by breaking the building mass up into a random assemblage of one-storey cubes. The individual apartments have been rendered as 'pixels', but whether this is how they are experienced remains to be seen.

Intermezzo, the apartment building behind Summertime on the north side of George Gershwinlaan, has an implicit horizontal articulation courtesy of the balcony floor slabs. The variety of design techniques employed to articulate the street frontage contributes to the street's informal, residential character.

DETAILS

1

3

2

4

Buffer for Housing

George Gershwinlaan's residential function is expressed in the street frontages. These are more or less explicitly designed, generally one to two storeys high and chiefly semi-active. There are occasional commercial uses, but the ground floors consist mainly of apartments and the main entrances to the apartment buildings.

The ground floor facades do not differ in materialization and design from the floors above. However, although the facades are not differentiated, a green buffer zone between the footpath and the street edge provides a degree of privacy to the occupants of the ground floor apartments. A clearly defined transitional zone has been created between street edge and street space using such small-scale elements as low walls, hedges, raised planters and the occasional small tree. The hedges reinforce the private nature of the ground floor and, as well as introducing a human scale and size into the street space, they form a refined, perfectly fitting barrier between residents and passers-by. Owing to the presence of outdoor spaces on various upper floors, the buildings provide plenty of visual contact with the street.

Fine Grain

The detailing and materialization of the buildings and the public space are fine-grained. Strips of a different type of paving create a 'soft' transition between building and street space and between private and public space. At the same time, these strips of paving and the raised planters, in the same material as the brick facades, connect the buildings with the street. The facade cladding consists chiefly of facade brickwork in different colours and textures. The small-scale elements, such as balconies with glass balustrades and raised planters, make for a fine-grained articulation of the urban mass.

BUILDING VOLUMES

GROUND FLOOR

STREET LEVEL

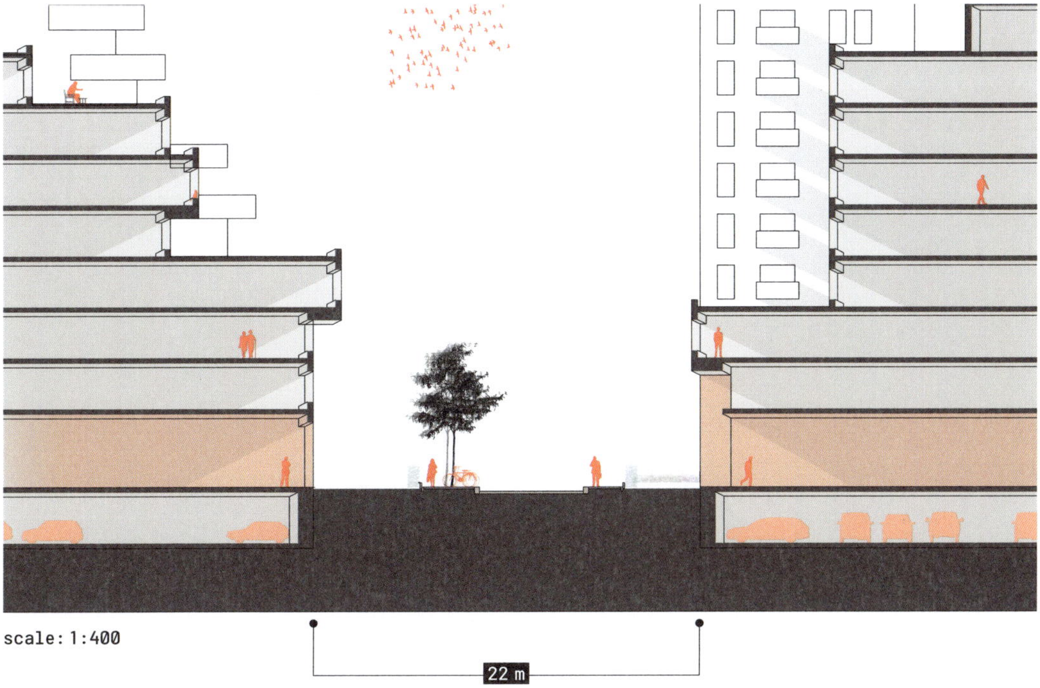

scale: 1:400

USER'S PERSPECTIVE

GUSTAV MAHLERLAAN

Gustav Mahlerlaan is an access road and as such has an important role to play in the efficient distribution of traffic. It is also the interface between the offices on its north side and the apartment buildings on its south side. This combination of uses gives the street a dual aspect: slick functional architecture on the north side, more solid brick architecture on its south side. At the rear the apartment buildings descend in tiers to the parallel George Gershwinlaan, in deference to its identity as a residential street with a human-scale streetscape. In Mahlerlaan and Gershwinlaan different design techniques have been employed that impact on the visual experience and scanpath. The tall office building volumes and taut street walls direct the eye to the end of the street where there is some traffic and pedestrians to be seen. A comparison of the effect of the two contrasting street walls indicates that the brick facades attract more fixations.

On the south side of Gustav Mahlerlaan the 'vertical bite' with recessed entrance captures the attention (see gazepath A), not least because of the otherwise black and sober facade. The recessed space also leads the eye upward. As such, this 'vertical bite' appears to break up the street wall at the level of the building and in so doing refines the rhythm introduced into this street of taut building volumes by the side streets. The adjacent building in the distance has a rounded corner the draws attention to the side street and invites exploration.

GEORGE GERSHWINLAAN

Something similar can be seen on the side elevation of Summertime. Instead of a rounded corner, the architects opted for cube-shaped balconies in white brick, finished with pink balcony railings. The windows and balconies are so conspicuous that they immediately capture the attention, after which the eye swiftly moves to the side street (see gazepath B). The gazepaths also reveal that from here the eye travels to the adjacent building, 900 Mahler, where it unerringly settles on the coffee bar entrance. In addition to being terminated by a band, the three-storey podium itself is clearly articulated in brickwork. Indeed, this type of street front attracts more visual contact than a fully transparent, active front that offers little for the eye to fasten on to.

There was much less interest in the opposite street front, in part because it is largely obscured by the foliage of the medium-sized trees. The street frontage and the awnings did attract a few fixations (see gazepath C).

In the George Gershwinlaan, the fixations tended to be more dispersed, across the full width of the street profile. The design technique of a tiered elevation before the building rises to its full height visually restricts the street space to those first three to four levels (see gazepath D). They also attract the most fixations. It seems that the design principle employed here does indeed succeed in making the street wall appear to be lower than it actually is. In the visual analysis it can be seen that people distinguish and

GUSTAV MAHLERLAAN

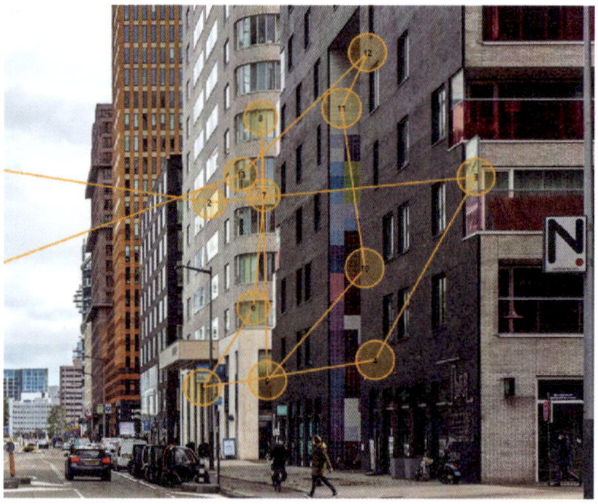

A Focus on the 'vertical bite' with recessed entrance and on the windows of the rounded corner of the adjoining building.

B The balconies and the active street front with coffee bar attract attention.

C Trees mask the street frontage. Fixations confined to prominent signs.

GEORGE GERSHWINLAAN

D Street wall 'read' as four storeys high.

E Individual windows and balconies are scanned in an upward movement.

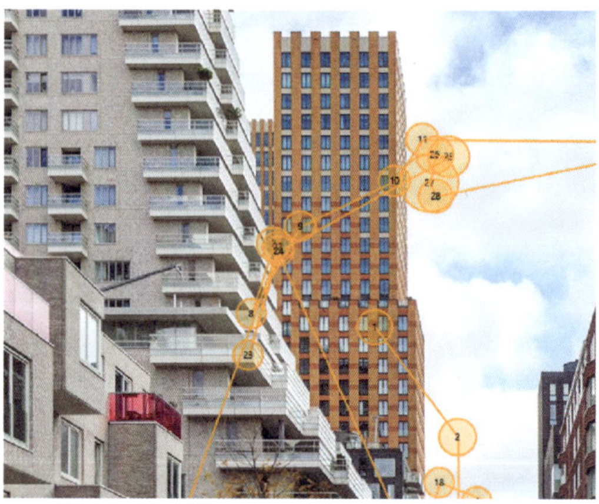

F Extensive scanning of tower in the background via the tiered buildings in the foreground.

'read' the cube-shaped volumes individually. Thus the apartments represent the human scale for the users (see gazepath E) and strengthen the relationship between inside and outside and between private and public.

The Summertime apartment complex and the Intermezzo complex beyond it both descend in tiers to the street producing a layered perspective with views of the buildings behind. The strong vertical articulation of the Symphony 1 tower attracts eye fixations to the building's contours and lends depth to the street wall.

AMSTERDAM / ZUIDAS

CONCLUSION

Originally conceived as a monofunctional financial centre, today the Zuidas boasts a rich mix of living and working. The ultimate aim is to turn it into a pedestrian-friendly, highly urban liveable environment – a place where families will also feel at home and want to live.

The neuroarchitecture analysis shows that in Gustav Mahlerlaan various design techniques have been used in an attempt to soften the junction between the tall street walls and the street space. They include awnings and (partially) set back buildings. Visually, such interventions appear to have been successful, but in many places the transition from high-rise to street space is fairly hard. Attempts by retailers and restaurant owners to soften the transition by placing planters on either side of the street seemed to go unnoticed by the participants. The difference in scale would appear to be too great to be bridged in this way. The street received an average rating compared with other streets in the study, which is not bad for a traffic corridor.

A very different approach to scaling has been adopted on George Gershwinlaan. The building mass on this street steps back quite markedly, making it seem as though the street wall is no more than three to four storeys high. This is reflected in the recorded eye movements of test participants. These staggered setbacks, in combination with the cube-shaped, individually recognizable apartments, facilitate contact and connection and in so doing counteract the anonymity that is often a feature of high-rise areas. The use of greenery as the transition between street edge and street space helps to create an intimate, small-scale streetscape appropriate to a residential setting. It was highly rated by the participants and ended in third place out of all twelve streets.

CONNECT
RBC

5 – DESIGN SOLUTIONS

HUMANIZING DENSIFICATION

The question we set out to answer in this book using a combination of research through design and neuroarchitecture, is which design solutions can help to achieve a human scale in streets in (new) areas of high-rise. Architecture, urban design and landscape architecture already have at their disposal a wealth of design techniques for creating attractive living environments, but most of those techniques have their origins in a quite different era or setting.

In our study of twelve streets in six different cities we have shown which combinations of these solutions appear to work in different highly densified situations, and which do not. Having analysed each of the twelve streets individually, in this chapter we synthesize the main lessons and conclusions.

Looking at all the streets in the neuroarchitecture analyses, what patterns emerge and what practical lessons and insights can we draw from them for achieving a human scale in high-rise areas? The effective patterns are visible at different levels of scale, from the urban design basis, the massing and the design of the street up to its junction with the buildings, to the subtle, fine-grained details. Our study was based on peoples' eye-level perspective and response to the street. This put the focus on urban design and the architectural solutions employed in the street space, whether mandated or specially designed for that space. Not all of them, of course, but certainly the solutions that make themselves felt at eye level, for that is the perspective that ultimately determines the shape of the living environment.

HEIGHT-WIDTH RATIO OF THE STREET

Let's start with an overview of the height-width ratio of the twelve streets [FIG. 5.1]. According to the classic patterns developed by Alexander et al. (1977, p. 490) a street works best for pedestrians when its width is no more than the height of the buildings lining it. If we look at the cross-sections and height-width ratios of the streets we can see big differences. For example, the street space in Sjøgangen (1:4.5) and Atkinson Street (1:5.5) is very enclosed, yet the buildings are not so very tall.

Compare that with Toronto's Wellington Street West (1:3.5) where the buildings rise to some 260 metres (853 feet). The largely unbroken wall of high-rise buildings, which stand directly on the street, contribute to a 'non-human' scale. This is intensified by the narrow pedestrian strip that stands in stark contrast to the street space the large buildings are allowed to occupy with raised and partly screened outdoor seating, and the four lanes of traffic. The scanpath here is much more searching, a sign that the space offers few (visual) points of reference.

In Amsterdam's Gustav Mahlerlaan we see something interesting. There the bulk of the building volumes has been broken up in a variety of ways, including a triple-height street frontage and a six-storey incision to mark an entrance. These are giant measures, almost as if they were made for 'the giant'. But we can also see that interventions like this that break up the visual bulk of the volumes have a positive effect on the human scale. This can be further amplified by the detailing of the street front, by a coherent, wide space for pedestrians and a separate lane for slow traffic that keeps motorized traffic at a safe distance.

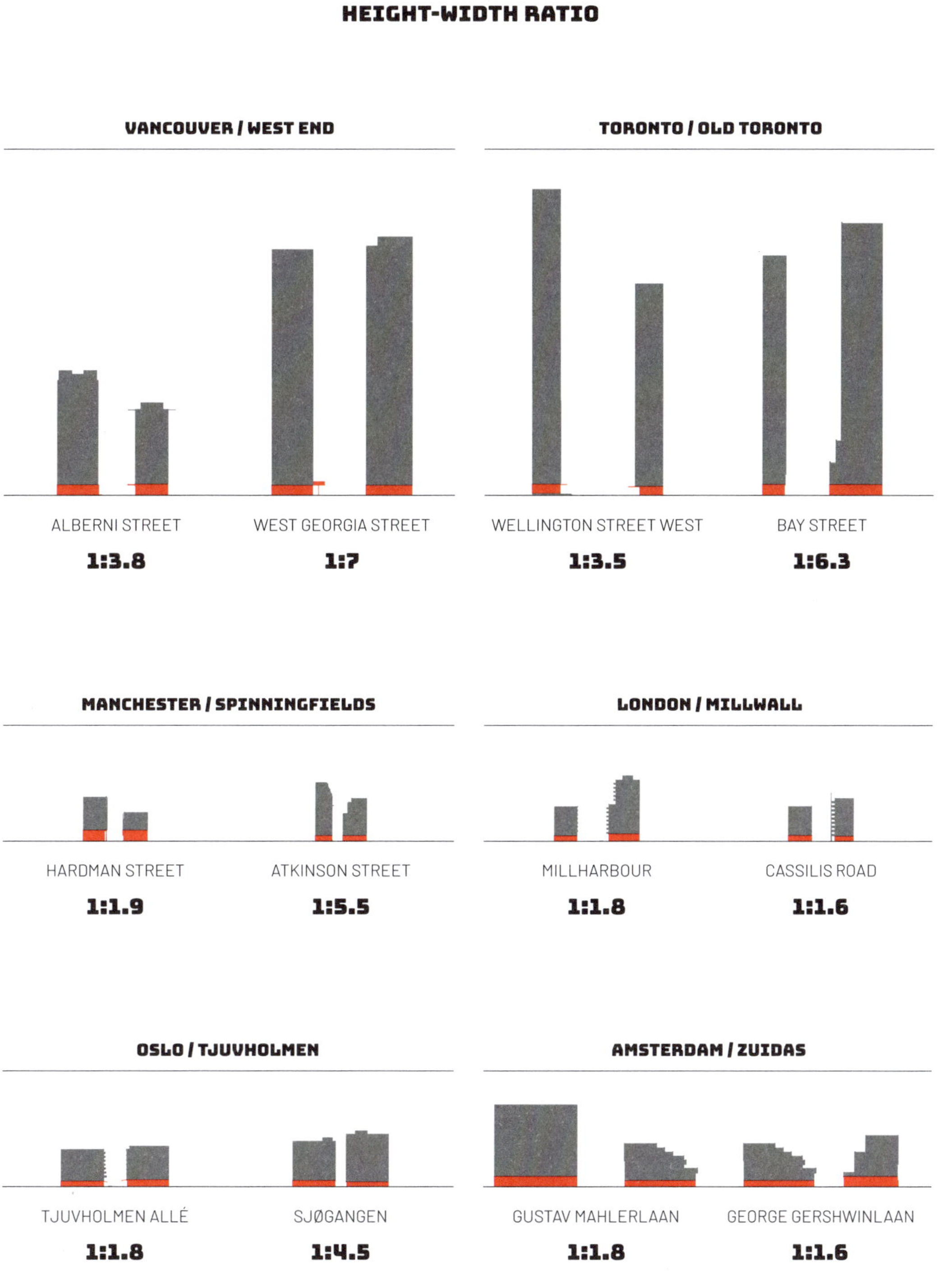

FIG. 5.1 Height to width ratio.

FIG. 5.2 Wellington Street West

FIG. 5.3 George Gershwinlaan

FIG. 5.4 Tjuvholmen Allé

SCALING VOLUMES

Scaling is a key means of mitigating high density and especially high-rise vis-à-vis the user at street level. In this respect the contrast between Wellington Street West in Toronto [FIG. 5.2] and George Gershwinlaan in the Amsterdam's Zuidas [FIG. 5.3] borders on caricature.

The high-rise in Toronto lands on the street edge without mediation; it is direct and uncompromising, and this is reinforced by the substantial entrance stairs and a functional materialization that has an almost hypnotic effect as the repetitive pattern extends skywards.
On George Gershwinlaan the high-rise steps back in elegant and rhythmical tiers, as if intent on allowing the street as much space as possible at eye level.

Another solution altogether is on display in Tjuvholmen Allé [FIG. 5.4]. Here the scaling is achieved by a strong connection between buildings by means of a pronounced horizontal articulation and between continuous street walls and the narrow street space. In all three cases clear and straightforward decisions have been made.

FIG. 5.5 West Georgia Street

FIG. 5.6 Bay Street

FIG. 5.7 Millharbour

FIG. 5.8 George Gershwinlaan

FIG. 5.9 Alberni Street

Between these two extremes are the streets where more stand-alone scaling design solutions have been applied, such as the urban layer in West Georgia Street in Vancouver [FIG. 5.5] and the sculptural alternation of the indented building envelope in Bay Street, the other studied street in Toronto [FIG. 5.6]. The outcome of such in-between variants is a less coherent and legible street-scape for the pedestrian. That is reflected in the eye-movement patterns and evaluations of the participants. More clear-cut and consistently applied choices in coherent design solutions were rated positively.

TOWERS HAVE AN IMPACT AT EYE LEVEL AS WELL

One of the important findings of the neuroarchitecture tests is that towers have an impact on eye level experience as well. However much attention is paid to eye level in the design, the decor of the towers above eye level is a real and essential part of the visual field. From London's Millharbour where high-rise buildings toe the property line [FIG. 5.7] and Amsterdam's George Gershwinlaan [FIG. 5.8], where the staggered setbacks offer a view of the towers, to Vancouver's Alberni Street [FIG. 5.9] where the towers are partially screened by awnings, setbacks and trees: in all cases the towers invariably enter the participants' visual field.

FIG. 5.10 Wellington Street West

FIG. 5.11 Sjøgangen

FIG. 5.12 Bay Street

This applies equally to tall towers whose designers have resorted to setbacks or podium construction in an effort to hide them from view. From the footpath the towers on the other side of the street are visible and sometimes those in the distance on the same side as the viewer as well. The design of the tower and its 'crown' is consequently about more than the silhouette of the city from a distance. The strictly functional, abstract towers that seem to be detached from their podiums in accordance with Vancouverism principles, do not work as expected. This raises new questions regarding the design of upper floors and the materialization of towers in relation to the human scale and experience at eye level. How many 'pixels' are visible from a distance and what are the implications in terms of size and scale for the design task?

PERSPECTIVE AND DEPTH

As part of the pedestrian's visual field perspective, towers lend depth to the street space. But there are more perspectival effects at work here. Once again Toronto's Bay Street and Wellington Street West [FIG. 5.10] are almost caricatural, in this instance with respect to the building line. The deviations are extreme: deeply set back in some places, elsewhere extending almost to the kerb. This is reflected in eye fixations on the buildings that 'emerge' from behind, literally stepping into the visual field. In places where the building line is set back there is more space and air in the street, but those places are not visible from a distance.

In the case of shorter streets, like Oslo's Sjøgangen [FIG. 5.11], the building at the end of the street plays an important role in perspective and experience. With such a short street, the building is not only clearly visible, it also completes the street. Our eye-tracking data shows that this building received considerable attention. Accordingly, the design of that building has as much impact on the quality, attractiveness and role of Sjøgangen as a connecting cross street, as the design and layout of the street itself.

FIG. 5.13 Tjuvholmen Allé

FIG. 5.14 Atkinson Street

The Sjøgangen example is a variant of Kevin Lynch's landmark principle: a distinctive or characteristic building or object occupying a central position in the visual field plays a key role in the navigation, identity and experience of a place (see for example Banerjee & Southworth 1990). There are several variants of the principle on show in this study. A traditional variant is the clock tower on Toronto's Bay Street [FIG. 5.12]. Owing to both its design and its central position in the streetscape it dictates the perspective, helps potential pedestrians get their bearings and ties streets together. The eye-movement patterns reveal how the gaze lands on it.

A similar lesson can be drawn from Oslo's Tjuvholmen Allé [FIG. 5.13]. There the building line is taut and there is a strong emphasis on the eye-level perspective, with double-height ground floors, raised entrance areas, differentiation in paving tiles and subtly 'undulating' frontages. The scanpath here is horizontal and scarcely rises above the tops of the trees. The horizontal articulation in the facades and street space guide the eye to the end of the street where there is a relatively taller building flanked by two lower buildings. Together they form a small public square.

In addition to offsets in the building line and landmarks, the perspective can also be affected by a slight curve in the street. This is evident in Manchester's Atkinson Street, which makes a gentle turn to the right in the viewpoint chosen for this study [FIG. 5.14]. Via the gentle curve and horizontal facade bands the gaze is automatically drawn to the building in the distance. Moreover, the building line is set back at the bend allowing the most distant building to be seen, lending perspective to the view and assisting navigation. When there is a slight bend in a street, the buildings along that curve present a design challenge that is crucial to the quality of the streetscape at eye level.

FIG. 5.15 Cassilis Road

FIG. 5.16 Millharbour

RHYTHM IN THE STREET

The composition of the volumes affects the rhythm of the street and so also the visual experience. Several variants can be seen in the twelve streets in the study. Take London's Isle of Dogs. Cassilis Road [FIG. 5.15] exudes an almost suburban atmosphere, with its unshowy architecture, a more classic composition, the low-traffic street space and a number of dwellings with hedged-in front gardens. The taut distribution of balconies draws the eye upwards.

A very different interpretation of rhythm and composition can be seen in Millharbour [FIG. 5.16]. On the one hand the buildings along the street rise steeply in height (from the chosen viewpoint). On the other hand the specific expressions of individual buildings provide the street with identity and rhythm. The building with a facade of randomly placed balconies is particularly important for the rhythm of the street while also generating connections. As the eye-movement patterns reveal, the eye is led gradually upwards via the active ground floor to the French balconies and from there to the facade with the randomly placed balconies, where it 'lingers'. The high-rise building visible in the distance 'rounds off the visual field'.

DIFFERENTIATION OF THE STREET FRONT

One of the more traditional historical design techniques entails the differentiation of the ground floor. Interestingly, this principle is barely used in the modern architecture of the streets in the study. The street wall descends to ground level with very little in the way of differentiation. In London's Cassilis Road, for example, although the lower floors are differently arranged and framed, in the eye-movement patterns of the participants it is clear that they form a single entity with the floors above.

FIG. 5.17 Hardman Street

FIG. 5.18 Atkinson Street

Manchester's Hardman Street [FIG. 5.17] shows how an almost identical composition can have quite a different outcome. All the buildings there have a transparent ground floor, whereas the volumes above have a single type of cladding: on one side glazed panelling, on the other perforated facade panelling. There is no parcellation and the overall effect is functional. This results in a relatively rapid eye-movement pattern. The emphasis may be on eye level, yet the Y-shaped columns soon lead the eye upwards. The gaze then darts to the other side only to drift down again to the entrances, the trees and other elements at eye level.

ACTIVATING THE EDGES

In urban design practice the creation of an active street front is an important means of humanizing the street at eye level. Building upon Jane Jacobs' 'eyes on the street' concept, the importance of an active street front is today universally acknowledged. The streets in the study exhibit many variations on the theme, with varying effects on people's visual behaviour.

Transparency alone does not make a street front active. In Manchester's Hardman Street, for example, those parts of the street front where there is genuine activity to be seen attract attention, whereas the transparent sections, which are concealed behind privacy film, are only fleetingly scanned.
Architecture plays a vital role here, too. On Manchester's Atkinson Street [FIG. 5.18] the modern building with a glazed ground floor and restaurant is much more active than the rear elevation of the historic Sunlight House. Nevertheless, after resting briefly on the glazed frontage the viewer's gaze darts to the other side of the street, which is examined in detail. Clearly, for a street front to be perceived as active, other factors come into play. People look to where people might be expected to be, while posters, images and text are noted automatically.

FIG. 5.19 Cassilis Road

FIG. 5.20 George Gershwinlaan

FIG. 5.21 Gustav Mahlerlaan

Streets with ground-floor dwellings also attract attention. In London's Cassilis Road [FIG. 5.19] participants tried to look into ground-floor verandas, which in turn serves to reminds us that protective measures are required in high-density housing situations like this. In Cassilis Road the street-level dwellings are located on a raised ground floor and set back behind front gardens. An added layer of privacy is provided by street trees, which filter views into the dwellings.

The housing along Amsterdam's George Gershwinlaan [FIG. 5.20] is also protected by greenery. At the same time, the individual balconies are clearly visible as separate entities. Unlike the taut line of balconies along Cassilis Road, the Amsterdam balconies attract a steadier gaze, and the eye-movement pattern is less fleeting. Amsterdam's Gustav Mahlerlaan [FIG. 5.21] demonstrates how a housing programme above street level can also enhance the visual interest of the ground floor. The gaze travels upwards to the balconies after which it moves to the coffee bar and other street-level uses.

FIG. 5.22 Millharbour

FIG. 5.23 Wellington Street West

FIG. 5.24 Atkinson Street

FIG. 5.25 Sjøgangen

FIG. 5.26 Wellington Street West

The ground floors of most of buildings on this street have a public function such as a supermarket or other retail outlet, or they form the entrance to offices. Of lesser but still considerable importance to eye-movement patterns is the visual accessibility of the street frontage. For example, those in London's Millbarbour (supermarket) [FIG. 5.22] and Toronto's Wellington Street West (offices) [FIG. 5.23] attract minimal attention because they are hidden deep beneath an overhang of the building.

Design solutions at eye level must also suit the speed, movement and perspective of the pedestrian. The street edge, also called transitional space, has a bearing on the link between the building and the street space. In very narrow streets, like Manchester's Atkinson Street [FIG. 5.24] and Oslo's Sjøgangen [FIG. 5.25], there is scarcely room for a layered transition. In the two Toronto streets [FIG. 5.26] there is plenty of room, but the means employed, such as entrance stairs and a concrete wall, are not so much a connection with the street as a brazen demarcation of the (semi-)private domain. It attracts very few eye fixations.

FIG. 5.27 George Gershwinlaan

FIG. 5.28 Tjuvholmen Allé

FIG. 5.29 Atkinson Street

FIG. 5.30 George Gershwinlaan

At the other end of the spectrum are Amsterdam's George Gershwinlaan [FIG. 5.27] and Oslo's Tjuvholmen Allé [FIG. 5.28], where there is a layered transition between public and private. In Tjuvholmen Allé the street space is divided up into a succession of individual parts. There is also differentiation in the pavement, with a larger paving tile used for pedestrian through-traffic and a smaller version close to the doors and the street edge. Together this generates a fan-shaped eye-movement pattern.

DETAILING AND COLOUR AT STREET LEVEL

Eye-level detailing plays a key role in architecture. The degree and scale of detailing determine the extent of 'softening'. A striking example of this is Atkinson Street [FIG. 5.29] in Manchester where the receding and projecting window frames and front doors of Sunlight House have a subtle layering effect. The glazed frontage on the other side of the street does almost the opposite with its lack of detailing and ornament and this contrast is reflected in the eye-movement patterns. Participants looked briefly at the glazed facade, but it was the detailing of the historical Sunlight House's facade that held their gaze. Thus the quality of the street at eye level is determined by such attention to details and subtle layering.

FIG. 5.31 Bay Street

FIG. 5.32 Alberni Street

The opposite occurs when the detailing is not subtle, such as the deep reveals and the hard, indented street walls in the Canadian Bay and West Georgia streets, which failed to hold the gaze.

The use of colour is another striking feature of these modern city streets, with most designers opting for more neutral colours like dark grey. Colour can be independent of the material, as in Oslo, or material and colour can coincide, as in the distinctively coloured brick used in Manchester. The effect of colour on eye-movement patterns can be seen with the Zuidas balconies [FIG. 5.30]. There it is the combination of colour with the design of discrete residential units that attracts attention. How entire coloured facade surfaces affect the eye-movement patterns and human scale needs further investigation.

Eye-movement patterns also reveal a functional reading of the street space. Posters, business signs, entrance door panels, logos, street maps and other street furniture attract attention. Almost as dominant as the interest in the presence of other people, is the invariable attention paid to moving and parked cars. It is possible that this is related to safety and our instinct to anticipate risk.

HUMAN DELIMITATION OF SPACE

Architectural elements play a subtle but essential role in our experience of a street, especially in high-rise situations. In Toronto, for example, the Arcade [FIG. 5.31] acts as a natural visual frame. We see something similar in the suburban row housing in Vancouver in the role played by concrete awnings [FIG. 5.32]. When street walls are much higher than this, an overhang ceases to be effective. At that point it is mainly balconies that create visual interest by breaking up the street walls into individual dwellings. Moreover, balconies are places where people are likely to be spotted.

FIG. 5.33 West Georgia Street

FIG. 5.34 Alberni Street

Architectural stylistic choices can also have a negative effect at street level. In Vancouver [FIG. 5.33] the set-back windows and deep reveals prevent pedestrians from seeing that part of the street front until they are right in front of it, thereby reducing the interaction between pedestrian and building.

The street profile of Vancouver's Alberni Street [FIG. 5.34] reveals that despite the contrast in grain and height, there is a degree of alignment between the two street edges. The awning on the apartment tower is about the same height as the roof of the row houses opposite, so that together they shape the street space. The profile also shows how the street design has created a soft transition from public to private space. Eye-movement patterns reflect how design elements like awnings create a visual demarcation at eye level.

Regardless, awnings and trees play a key role in the street at eye level. Awnings often literally obscure the view of the high-rise building, at least of that part of the high-rise directly above the awning. In addition to their screening function, awnings also provide rhythm and a horizontal accent to the street space. In Vancouver the awnings help to make the rhythm of the series of towers less visible at eye level.

Trees and other green elements also play a key role in eye-movement patterns. An absence of trees, as in Sjøgangen [FIG. 5.35], makes a street with high-rise seem hard, something that is not easy to mitigate with detailing at ground level, although the layering in Sjøgangen and the wealth of detailing in the facade of the older Sunlight House in Manchester's Atkinson Street provide some compensation.

FIG. 5.35 Sjøgangen

FIG. 5.36 Millharbour

Trees, like awnings, can have the effect of delimiting (scaling) and filtering (softening high-rise), but they also play another role. Trees add layering to the streetscape with the rustle of leaves and sound of birdsong [FIG. 5.36]. Trees also provide seasonal variation. Streets that include natural elements connect people with nature and are beneficial to human health (see Chapter 3 and Ulrich 1984).

SOLUTIONS AT AREA LEVEL

Although different in nature from the urban design and building level, quality at area level is also important. When density and use are high, the high-rise intrusive and the traffic, crowds, movement and noise relentless, the human scale becomes the opposite: a 'refuge' offering respite. A place where human beings can recharge and relax. In such situations some compensation may be possible at area level.

In Vancouver's West End, for example, the height-width ratio of West Georgia Street is an overwhelming 1:7. Wherever you look, there are towers with an abstract, functional design. Apart from various interventions at street level, an environment like this might be partially compensated at a different level of scale. Take Old Toronto. Directly behind the busy Bay and Wellington West streets are more sheltered inner or in-between areas. Naturally, the quality and accessibility of such (green) pause places is critical. How and whether this actually works requires further investigation.

FINAL WORD

Today, maybe for the first time since the major transitions at the end of the nineteenth century, building projects provide us with a new opportunity to rethink the fundamental premise of our cities and to make a structural leap in living quality. Our cities need to become more resistant to climate change and to include nature in their design. This would mean fewer cars on our streets and that alone would radically alter our view of public space. Our visual experience of our current urban environment offers lessons for successfully giving shape to these new building needs in the design.

The analysis of the neuroarchitecture tests regarding the twelve streets in the study shows how we rapidly scan the urban environment and attempt to process the information gained. In some streets that is not always easy owing to their design. Human beings are evolutionarily programmed to search for places where people might be for both social and safety reasons, but high-rise areas where the view is obstructed are not easy to read and understand. In our study we also saw how the architecture of the buildings and the street space is able to manage complexity. A judicious mix of design solutions like rhythm and variety can generate visual patterns and lend significance to buildings and other elements in the street space. That makes it easier for our senses to take in the situation and for our brains to process that sensory information.

A judicious mix of design solutions, such as rhythm and variety, can generate visual patterns and lend significance to buildings and other elements in the street space.

In our analyses we have seen how certain design solutions help pedestrians to connect with buildings and street spaces. They guide the eye and so help the pedestrian on their way. They make street-level functions like restaurants and entrances visible. Architecture can stimulate curiosity and fascination or, conversely, discourage it with a complex or monotonous design. The challenge facing cities today is to make the process of densification with a multitude of different spatial requirements and tall buildings both human and attractive.

As we have shown, neuroarchitecture provides the missing knowledge and technology needed to actively improve the liveability of our urban environments based directly on user experience, perception and behaviour. The results show that, contrary to expectations, even the higher floors in high-rise buildings make up a substantial part of the visual experience at street level. Design solutions have been shown to be capable of steering the gaze upwards or to keeping it fixed on the ground floor. If professionals see precisely what users see, they will be able to design more effective solutions.

This study represents a first venture into the hybrid field of neuroarchitecture. Neuroarchitecture is still young, but the possibilities it opens up are promising. Technological and knowledge development are making rapid strides and we expect that before long user-friendly tools for spatial practice will come onto the market.

Development plans that involve the introduction of new high-rise typologies need access to more evidence-based information about the (latent) needs of the user early on in the design process. Taken together, the study areas in which the design solutions aimed at achieving a human scale were tested with neuroarchitecture offer an initial series of lessons for further urban development based on the user's perspective.

VANCOUVER / WEST END

ALBERNI STREET

WEST GEORGIA STREET

TORONTO / OLD TORONTO

WELLINGTON STREET WEST

BAY STREET

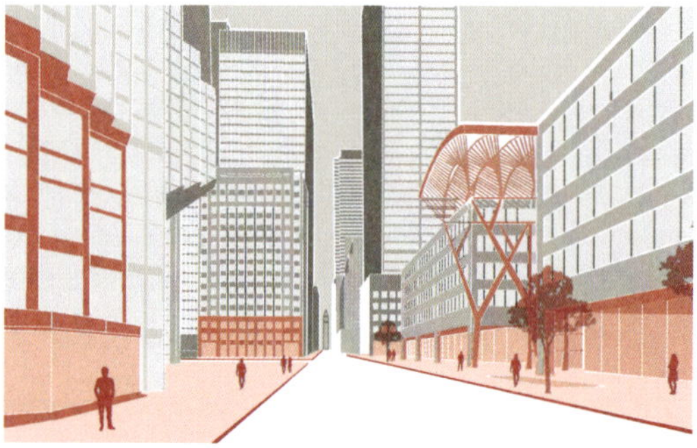

MANCHESTER / SPINNINGFIELDS

HARDMAN STREET

ATKINSON STREET

LONDON / MILLWALL

MILLHARBOUR

CASSILIS ROAD

OSLO / TJUVHOLMEN

TJUVHOLMEN ALLÉ

SJØGANGEN

AMSTERDAM / ZUIDAS

GUSTAV MAHLERLAAN

GEORGE GERSHWINLAAN

VANCOUVER / WEST END

ALBERNI STREET

WEST GEORGIA STREET

TORONTO / OLD TORONTO

WELLINGTON STREET WEST

BAY STREET

MANCHESTER / SPINNINGFIELDS

HARDMAN STREET

ATKINSON STREET

LONDON / MILLWALL

MILLHARBOUR

CASSILIS ROAD

OSLO / TJUVHOLMEN

TJUVHOLMEN ALLÉ

SJØGANGEN

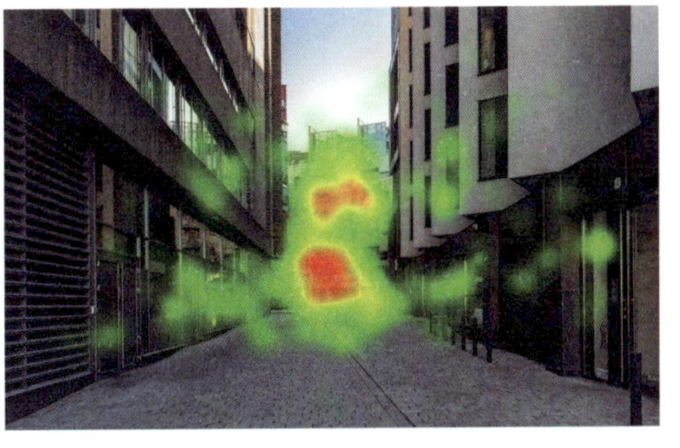

AMSTERDAM / ZUIDAS

GUSTAV MAHLERLAAN

GEORGE GERSHWINLAAN

VANCOUVER / WEST END

scale: 1:3000

ALBERNI STREET

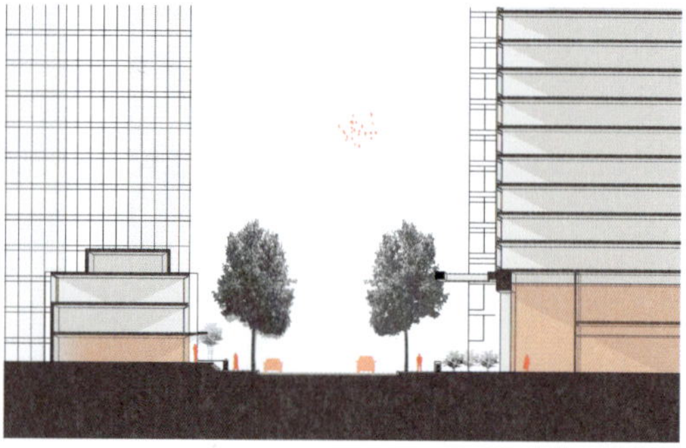

WEST GEORGIA STREET

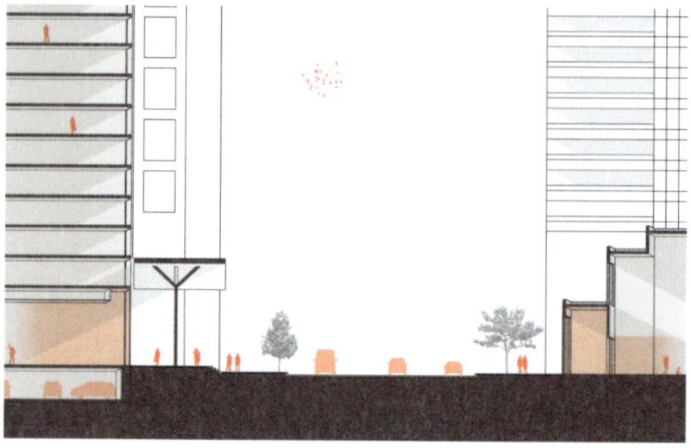

TORONTO / OLD TORONTO

scale: 1:3000

WELLINGTON STREET WEST

BAY STREET

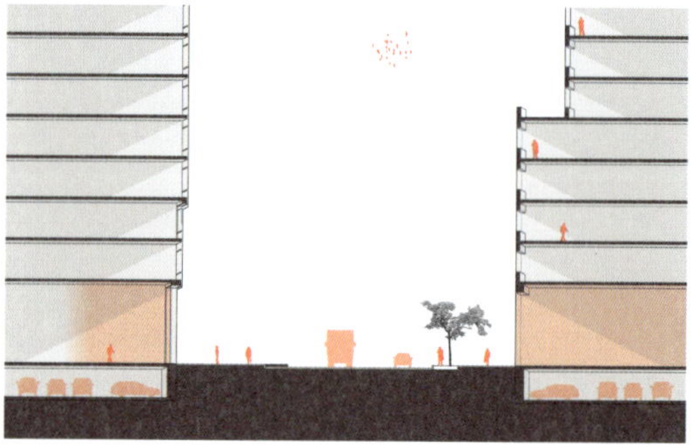

MANCHESTER / SPINNINGFIELDS

scale: 1:3000

HARDMAN STREET

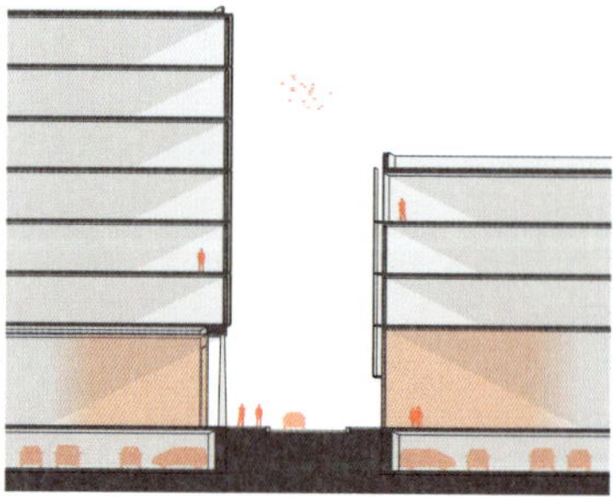

ATKINSON STREET

LONDON / MILLWALL

scale: 1:3000

MILLHARBOUR

CASSILIS ROAD

OSLO / TJUVHOLMEN

scale: 1:3000

TJUVHOLMEN ALLÉ

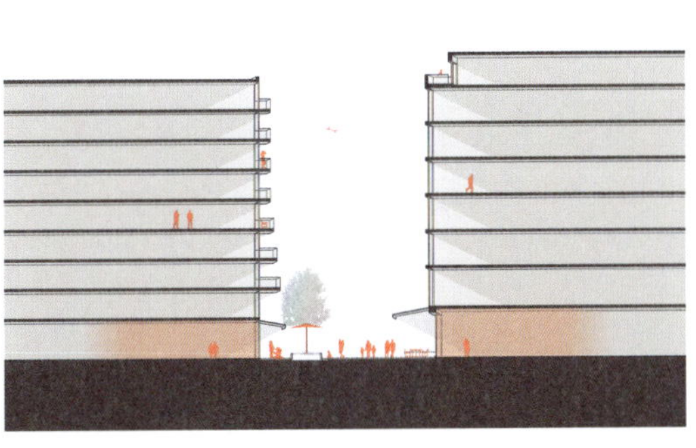

SJØGANGEN

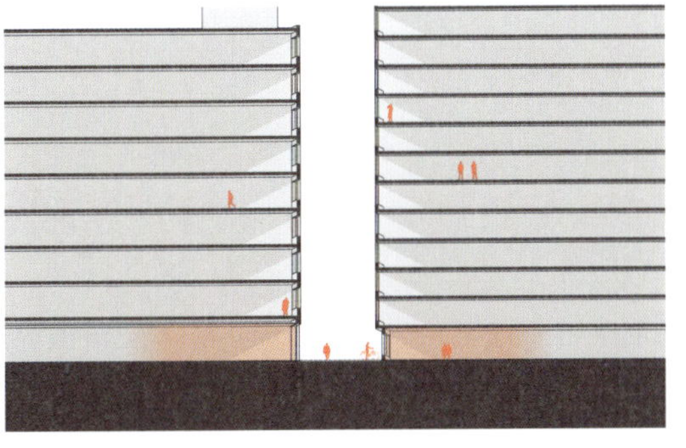

AMSTERDAM / ZUIDAS

scale: 1:3000

GUSTAV MAHLERLAAN

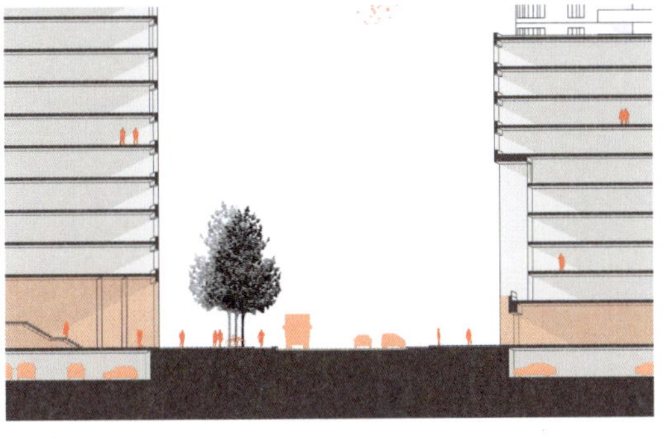

GEORGE GERSHWINLAAN

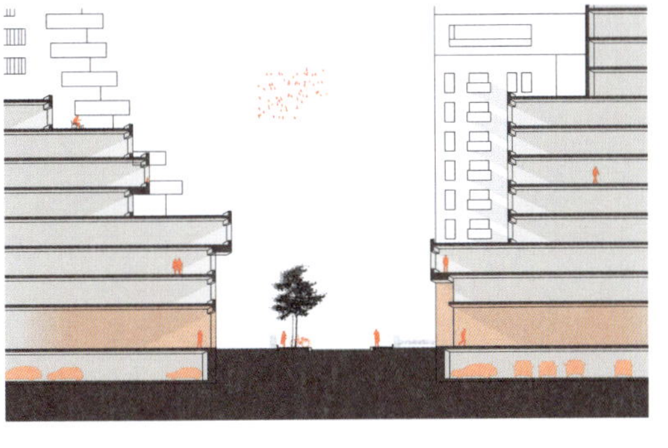

REFERENCES

Alexander, C., et al. (1977). *A Pattern Language. Towns, Buildings, Construction*, Oxford: Oxford University Press

Arends, E. (2023). *City Without Fear of Heights. The Development of a European High Rise Typology*. Rotterdam: nai010 publishers

Asgarzadeh, M., et al. (2012). 'Measuring Oppressiveness of Streetscapes', *Landscape and Urban Planning* 107, no. 1, pp. 1-11, doi:10.1016/j.landurbplan.2012.04.001

Banerjee, T., & M. Southworth (1990). *City Sense and City Design. Writings and Projects of Kevin Lynch*, Cambridge: MIT Press

Berg, A.E. Van Den, Y. Joye & S.L. Koole (2016), 'Why Viewing Nature is More Fascinating and Restorative than Viewing Buildings. A Closer Look at Perceived Complexity', *Urban Forestry & Urban Greening* 20, no. 1, pp. 397-401, doi:10.1016/j.ufug.2016.10.011

Bermudez, J., et al. (2017). 'Externally-induced Meditative States. An Exploratory fMRI Study of Architects' Responses to Contemplative Architecture', *Frontiers of Architectural Research* 6, no. 2, pp. 123-136, doi:10.1016/j.foar.2017.02.002

Berto, R., S. Massaccesi & M. Pasini (2008). 'Do Eye Movements Measured Across High and Low Fascination Photographs Differ? Addressing Kaplan's Fascination Hypothesis', *Journal of Environmental Psychology* 28, no. 2, pp. 185-191, doi:10.1016/j.jenvp.2007.11.004

Braudel, F. (1966, trans. 1972) *The Mediterranean and the Mediterranean World in the Age of Philip II*. New York: HarperCollins

Buswell, G.T. (1935). *How People Look at Pictures. A Study of the Psychology of Perception in Art*, Chicago: University of Chicago Press

Busquets, J., & D. Yang (2018). *Urban Grids. Handbook for Regular City Design*, Novato: Oro Editions

Chile, M.L., X.M. Black & C. Neill (2014). 'Experience and Expression of Social Isolation by Inner-city High-rise Residents', *Housing, Care and Support* 17, no. 3, pp. 151-166, dx.doi.org/10.1108/HCS-11-2013-0021

Cortinovis, C., D. Geneletti & D. Haase (2022). 'Higher Immigration and Lower Land Take Rates are Driving a New Densification Wave in European Cities', *npj Urban Sustainability* 2, no. 1. doi:10.1038/ s42949-022-00062-0

Dovey, K., & S. Wood (2015). 'Public/private Urban Interfaces. Type, Adaptation, Assemblage', *Journal of Urbanism: International Research on Placemaking and Urban Sustainability* 8, no. 1, pp. 1-16Ehinger, K.A., et al. (2009). 'Modelling Search for People in 900 Scenes. A Combined Source Model of Eye Guidance', *Visual Cognition* 17, nos. 6-7, pp. 945-978, doi:10.1080/13506280902834720.

Ellard, C. (2015). *Places of the Heart*, New York: Bellevue Literary Press

Franěk, M., et al. (2018). 'Differences in Eye Movements while Viewing Images with Various Levels of Restorativeness', *Journal of Environmental Psychology* 57, pp. 10-16, doi:10.1016/j.envp.2018.05.001

Gehl, J., L.J. Kaefer & S. Reigstad (2006). 'Close Encounters With Buildings', *Urban Design International* 11, pp. 29-47

Gehl, J. (2010). *Cities for People*, Washington: Island Press

Gehl, J. (2011). *Life Between Buildings. Using Public Space*, Washington: Island Press

Gehl, J., & B. Svarre (2013). *How to Study Public Life*, Washington: Island Press

Gemeente Amsterdam (2016). *Visie Zuidas 2016*, Gemeente Amsterdam, Amsterdam, zuidasbibliotheek.nl/visie-zuidas-2016

Gifford, R. (2007). 'The Consequences of Living in High-rise Buildings', *Architectural Science Review* 50, no. 1, pp. 1-16

Glaser, M. (ed.) (2012). *The City at Eye Level. Lessons for Street Plinths*, Delft: Eburon

Haas, T. (2008). *New Urbanism and Beyond. Designing Cities for the Future*, New York: Rizzoli

Henderson-Wilson, C. (2008). 'Inner City High-rise Living. A Catalyst for Social Exclusion and Social Connectedness', in A. Taket et al. (eds.), *Theorising Social Exclusion*, New York: Routledge

Hollander, J., G. Spanjar, A. Sussman, F. Suurenbroek & M. Wang (2022). 'Programming for the Subliminal Brain: Biometric Tools Reveal Architecture's Biological Impact', in: K. Menezes, P. De Oliveira-Smith & A.V. Woodworth (eds.), *Programming for Health and Wellbeing in Architecture*, Boston: Routledge, pp. 136-149, doi: 10.4324/9781003164418

Holmqvist, K., et al. (2011), *Eye Tracking. A Comprehensive Guide to Methods and Measures*. Oxford: Oxford University Press

Jacobs, A. (1995). *Great Streets*, Boston: MIT Press

Jacobs, J. (1961). *The Death and Life of Great American Cities*, New York: Random House

Jenkins, E. (2007). *To Scale. One Hundred Urban Plans*, New York: Routledge

Kaplan, R., & S. Kaplan (1989). *The Experience of Nature. A Psychological Perspective*, New York: Cambridge University Press

Kaplan, S. (1995). 'The Restorative Benefits of Nature. Toward an Integrative Framework', *Journal of Environmental Psychology* 15, no. 3, pp. 169-182, doi:10.1016/0272-4944(95)90001-2

Karandinou, A., & L. Turner (2017). 'Architecture and Neuroscience. What can the EEG recording of brain activity reveal about a walk through everyday spaces?', *International Journal of Parallel, Emergent and Distributed Systems* 32:sup1, S54-S65, doi:10.1080/17445760.2017.1390089

Karssenberg, H. et al. (2020). *Superplinten. Praktisch en beeldend handboek, Case study Sloterdijk, Zuid. In opdracht van de gemeente Amsterdam*, Amsterdam: STIPO and AM Gemeente Amsterdam

Luijten, A. (2002). 'Een modern sprookje. De Bijlmer in verandering/A Modern Fairy Tale. The Bijlmer Transforms', in D. van Hoogstraten & A. Jolles (eds.), *Amsterdam Zuidoost, Centrumgebied Zuidoost en stedelijke vernieuwing Bijlmermeer 1992-2010/In Amsterdam Southeast, Centre Area Southeast and the Renewal in the Bijlmermeer 1992-2010*, Bussum: Thoth, pp. 9-25

Lindal, P., & T. Hartig (2013). 'Architectural Variation, Building Height, and the Restorative Quality of Urban Residential Streetscapes', *Journal of Environmental Psychology* 33, pp. 26-36, doi:10.1016/j.jenvp.2012.09.003

Lynch, K. (1960). *The Image of the City*, Cambridge, MA: MIT Press

Mallgrave, H.F. (2013). *Architecture and Embodiment. The Implications of the New Sciences and Humanities for Design*, New York: Routledge

Nadal, M., et al. (2010). 'Visual Complexity and Beauty Appreciation. Explaining the Divergence of Results', *Empirical Study of the Arts* 28, no. 2, pp. 173-191, doi:10.2190/EM.28.2.d

Olszewska-Guizzo, A., et al. (2020). 'Can exposure to certain urban green spaces trigger frontal alpha asymmetry in the brain? Preliminary findings from a passive task EEG study', *International Journal of Environmental Research and Public Health* 17, no. 2, pp. 394. doi: 10.3390/ijerph17020394

Sassen, S. (2017). 'The Escalating Privatization of Urban Space Meets John Friedmann's Post-urban Landscape', in: H. Rangan et al., *Insurgencies and Revolutions. Reflections on John Friedmann's Contributions to Planning Theory and Practice*, New York: Routledge, 151-161

Sennett, R. (2018). *Building and Dwelling. Ethics for the City*, New York: Farrar, Straus and Giroux

Sim, D. (2019). Soft City, Washington: Island Press

Simpson, J. (2018). 'Street DNA. The who, where and what of visual engagement with the urban street', *Journal of Landscape Architecture* 13, no. 1, pp. 50-57

Simpson, J., et al. (2019a). 'Visual Engagement with Urban Street Edges. Insights Using Mobile Eye-tracking', *Journal of Urbanism. International Research on Placemaking and Urban Sustainability* 12, no. 3, pp. 259-278

Simpson, J., K. Thwaites & M. Freeth (2019b). 'Understanding Visual Engagement with Urban Street Edges along Non-Pedestrianised and Pedestrianised Streets Using Mobile Eye-Tracking', *Sustainability* 11, no. 15, pp. 42-51

Spanjar, G., & F. Suurenbroek (2020). 'Eye-Tracking the City. Matching the design of streetscapes in high-rise environments with users' visual experiences', *Journal of Digital Landscape Architecture* 5, pp. 374-385, doi:10.14627/537690038

Sussman, A., & J.B. Hollander (2015). *Cognitive Architecture Designing for How We Respond to the Built Environment*, New York: Routledge

Suurenbroek, F., I. Nio & M. de Waal (2019). *Responsive Public Spaces Exploring the Use of Interactive Technology in the Design of Public Spaces*, Amsterdam: AUAS, responsiveurbanspaces.amsterdam

Suurenbroek, F., & G. Spanjar (2018). '(Eye)Tracking Users' Patterns. Visual Experience and Choice Behavior in Transition Zones of Amsterdam-Southeast', *Proceedings of the Fourth Conference on Shared Behavioral Outcomes, ANFA 2018*, La Jolla, CA: Salk Institute

Suurenbroek, F., & G. Spanjar (2021). 'Exploring Eye-Tracking Technology. Assessing How the Design of Densified Built Environments Can Promote Inhabitants' Well-being', in J. Hollander & A. Sussman (eds.), *Urban Experience and Design. Contemporary Perspectives on Improving the Public Realm*, Boston: Routledge, pp. 91-103, 10.4324/9780367435585

Suurenbroek, F., & G. Spanjar (2021). *Sensing Streetscapes. Perspectieven op verdichting*, Amsterdam: HvA, www.building4wellbeing.com

Thwaites, K., A. Mathers & I. Simkins (2013). *Socially restorative Urbanism. The Theory, Process and Practice of Experiemics*, New York: Routledge

Thwaites, K., J. Simpson & I. Simkins (2020). 'Transitional Edges. A Conceptual Framework for Socio-spatial Understanding of Urban Street Edges', *URBAN DESIGN International*, pp. 1-15.

Ulrich, R.S. (1984). 'View Through a Window May Influence Recovery from Surgery', *Science* 224, pp. 417-419, doi:10.1126/sciences.6143402

Valtchanov, D., & C.G. Ellard (2015). 'Cognitive and Affective Responses to Natural Scenes: Effects of Low Level Visual Properties on Preference, Cognitive Load and Eyemovements', *Journal of Environmental Psychology* 43, pp. 184-195. doi:10.1016/j.jenvp.2015.07.001.

Wilson, E.O. (1984). *Biophilia*, Boston, MA: Harvard University Press

Wilson, E.O., & S.R. Kellert (1995). *The Biophilia Hypothesis*, Washington, DC: Island Press

CREDITS

TEXT
Frank Suurenbroek en Gideon Spanjar, with the collaboration of Kees Versluis

EDITING
Els Brinkman

TRANSLATION
Robyn de Jong-Dalziel

DESIGN + LAYOUT
Véro Crickx, Sirene Ontwerpers, Amsterdam

PHOTOGRAPHY (unless otherwise indicated)
Roos Aldershoff Fotografie [pp. 16-17], James Alfre (Vancouver) [pp. 56-57, 60, 64-64, 68, 201, 209, 210], Atelier Rijksbouwmeester [p. 3], Olivier van Breugel (Amsterdam) [pp. 4-5, 176-177, 180, 184-185, 188, 200, 201, 206, 208], David Burrows (Manchester) [pp. 104-105, 108, 112-113, 116, 203, 205, 207, 208], Lyske Gais de Bildt [pp. 28-29], © Google Earth [pp. 53, 77, 101, 125, 149, 173], Simon Kennedy (Londen) [pp. 128-129, 132, 136-137, 140, 201, 204, 206, 207, 210], Luuk Kramer [pp. 2-3], Arnaud Marthouret (Toronto) [pp. 80-81, 84, 88-89, 92, 200, 201, 202, 207, 209, 210], New Media Services [pp. 15, 44-45], Eric Rubens [p. 31], Gideon Spanjar [pp. 6-7], Bernat Tubau (Oslo) [pp. 152-153, 156, 160-161, 164, 200, 202, 203, 207, 208, 210], Wikimedia Commons [p. 32]

GRAPHS AND DRAWINGS (unless otherwise indicated)
Amsterdam University of Applied Sciences, Professorship of Spatial Urban Transformation

PRINTING
die Keure, Brugge

PRODUCTION
Marja Jager, nai010 publishers

PUBLISHER
Marcel Witvoet, nai010 publishers

ISBN 978-94-6208-788-0
NUR 648
BISAC ARC000000
THEMA AM

Neuroarchitecture. Designing High-rise Cities at Eye Level is also available in Dutch (*Neuroarchitectuur. Ontwerpen van hoogbouwsteden op ooghoogte*) and as an e-book: ISBN 978-94-6208–838-2

NAI010 PUBLISHERS

nai010 publishers is an internationally orientated publisher specialized in developing, producing and distributing books in the fields of architecture, urbanism, art and design.
www.nai010.com

nai010 books are available internationally at selected bookstores and from the following distribution partners:

- North, Central and South America - Artbook | D.A.P., New York, USA, dap@dapinc.com
- Rest of the world - Idea Books, Amsterdam, the Netherlands, idea@ideabooks.nl

For general questions, please contact nai010 publishers directly at sales@nai010.com or visit our website www.nai010.com for further information.

SENSING STREETSCAPES

This publication and the associated Sensing Streetscapes research are co-funded by the Dutch National taskforce for applied research SIA, a division of the Dutch Research Council (NWO) and the Faculty of Technology at the Amsterdam University of Applied Sciences.

Amsterdam University of Applied Sciences

SIA Regieorgaan

With thanks to all the researchers involved in the Sensing Streetscapes research project: Kees Versluis, Jolanda Tetteroo, Lyske Gais de Bildt, Zoë Jonker, Sába Schramkó, Nanda Piersma, Maarten Groen and Tom Otten.

Special thanks to Kees Versluis, Lyske Gais de Bildt, Sam Vink, Véro Crickx and Erik Prins for the development of the maps, drawings, heatmaps and other graphs.

We are grateful for the commitment of the Sensing Streetscapes consortium partners: Akka, AM, BNSP, Bureau Maris, de Levende Stad, Gemeente Amsterdam, IAA Architecten, iMoss, Nohnik (now Polyfern), OTO, OverMorgen, PosadMaxwan, Reuring Advies, Ruimte + Wonen, Space & Matter, Woningstichting Eigen Haard.

We also wish to thank the research project's scientific advisory panel: Stefano Andreani, Harvard University, Jordan Lacey, RMIT University, Justin Hollander and Ann Sussman, Tufts University, Marco te Brömmelstroet, UvA, Winnie Damen, TU Delft, Colin Ellard, University of Waterloo, Davide Ruzzon, Università di Venezia.